The California Gold Rush

Here's a true-life adventure story that recreates "the days of old, the days of gold" when young men went west with pick and shovel to look for riches and stayed to add a new chapter to our country's history.

The entire nation was caught up in gold fever as people from all walks of life dropped everything to search for a fortune. The people who made the early days of the West so colorful and exciting are skillfully brought to life: the explorers, the prospectors, the bandits, and the people who built fortunes not on gold itself but on the business it brought them. Many anecdotes about the fabulous "strikes" and legendary characters of the mining camps have been culled from old documents to supply fresh and authentic background. This is a fascinating account of a time when it seemed that anything could happen.

The California Gold Rush

By May McNeer

RANDOM HOUSE · NEW YORK

Library of Congress Cataloging-in-Publication Data:
McNeer, May Yonge. The California gold rush. (A Landmark book) SUMMARY: Traces the history of the gold rush in California including anecdotes about legendary characters and fabulous "strikes" of the mining camps. 1. California—Gold discoveries—Juvenile literature. 2. California—History—1846–1850—Juvenile literature. [1. California—Gold discoveries. 2. California—History—1846–1850] I. Title. F865.M4 1987 979.4 87-4685 ISBN: 0-394-89177-5 (pbk.); 0-394-90306-4 (lib. bdg.)

Manufactured in the United States of America 1 2 3 4 5 6 7 8 9 0

Contents

The
California
Gold Rush

1

"It's Gold!"

The early morning sun gleamed like a bright golden coin above the California foothills. It was January 24, 1848. In all the green wilderness world there was no sign of life except a wisp of smoke from a breakfast fire, and the figure of a man walking beside a ditch that led from a nearly finished sawmill to a river. Suddenly he stopped and stared intently down.

James Marshall was a surly man, without friends, and he was a long way from his old home in New Jersey. The other men at Sutter's Fort thought him a little odd, and stupid. But he was the only millwright in all the California country, and a good mechanic as well.

He looked up at the mill he was building for John Sutter, the German-Swiss owner of this big landed estate, and he felt satisfied. The mill was coming along well, the dam was finished, and the tailrace, or ditch, to let water back into the American River, was dug out. Each night Marshall opened the gate to allow the water to wash as much gravel and sand down the tail-race as possible. Then in the early morning he went there to see how it looked.

Before long this mill, the first in the new territory, would be sawing lumber to ship down the Sacramento River to the village of San Francisco.

James Marshall glanced down again. Something had caught his eye. What was it? He leaned forward. Something glittered a little in the gravel against a stone. He sat on one heel and picked up the little glittering lump that felt strangely heavy.

Gold! Could it be gold?

The small piece looked more like brass. It was no larger than a tiny dried pea. He rubbed it. It still looked golden.

James Marshall stood up and saw his laborers sitting around their fire drinking coffee and eating flapjacks. Beyond them the Indian workers moved quietly, preparing their breakfast of dried deer meat. Marshall walked slowly to the fire, where his sober Mormon workers ate silently, and opened his hand.

"I found it in the tailrace."

The men stopped chewing and one exclaimed, "Fool's gold," and laughed.

Another spit carefully into a bush several yards away. " 'Tain't nothing but iron pyrite," he said. "Fool's gold, that's all."

The first man took a closer look, reached for another flapjack, and said, "That's right. That stuff fools lots of people." They all grinned knowingly at each other.

James Marshall scowled and clenched his fist over the little pebble. Did they think he was a fool? He turned on his heel and strode up the slope to a small log cabin where smoke was lazily rising from an adobe (clay) chimney.

As he approached he saw Elizabeth Wimmer, wife of his foreman, standing with a long stick in hand over a big black soap kettle. Elizabeth Wimmer was one of the few American women in this land so lately taken from Mexico. She had refused to be left at Sutter's Fort when Peter, her husband, went to take charge of the

Indian laborers building the sawmill.

As Marshall came up to her he growled, "Look here, Mrs. Wimmer. This looks like gold. The men say it's iron pyrite." He unclenched his fist.

Mrs. Wimmer leaned forward curiously. Then, before he could stop her, she picked up the little piece and dropped it into the bubbling soap kettle. "We'll soon find out, Mr. Marshall. If it isn't gold, the lye in this kettle will eat it up quick."

James Marshall said nothing, but turned and went back to the breakfast he had not yet eaten.

That night as he went to the cabin where he lived with the Wimmers he felt confident again. The mill would work well with the tailrace deepened. He was thinking of the lumber they would soon be sawing and of the money they could get for it in the sleepy village of San Francisco.

As he sat and smoked his pipe he was startled by Mrs. Wimmer. Through the door she marched, and up to the scrubbed pine table.

"There!" she cried triumphantly. "It's gold all right, Mr. Marshall!"

She flung on the table the heavy little stone. In the light of the candle it glowed and gleamed. Marshall picked it up, then put it on the floor, grasped a rock lying by the hearth, and hammered the stone with it. It didn't break. Gold!

Next morning at dawn he went back to the tailrace. From cracks between the boulders he picked up more of the tiny gold pieces. Carefully he stowed them away in a small buckskin bag and went back to his job of getting the mill going. But that night he could scarcely sleep. Through his slow brain a shower of glittering flakes seemed to fall like sparks.

The following day he announced to Peter Wimmer, "Supplies are getting low. I'm going to the fort for grub. Wimmer, you take over while I'm gone."

Peter Wimmer glanced at his wife but said nothing.

Down through the beautiful California country Marshall rode to Sutter's Fort. As he came closer he glanced at the herds of cattle browsing on the lush grass. He nodded when Sutter's Mexican cowhands, the vaqueros, called out friendly greetings, waving their high sombreros. He didn't fancy these guitar strummers with their jingling boots and brilliant scarlet-and-yellow serapes flung over their shoulders.

The fort was the only American stronghold in the territory. John Sutter had obtained land from Mexico. He had been loyal to that country until California was practically taken over by the United States toward the end of the Mexican War. But now he was in sympathy with America. His fort was at the California end of the only wagon trail from the States, and he gave aid and work to any Americans who came that way.

Now as Marshall rode through the gateway in the adobe walls surrounding Sutter's Fort, he seemed to enter a city in itself. Here were shops and sheds and houses. He heard the clang-clang of a blacksmith's hammer on an anvil, and the soft Spanish song of a Mexican woman as she slapped tortillas on a flat stone.

Marshall strode at once to Sutter's house, and startled his boss with his air of excitement.

"What is this, Mr. Marshall?" asked John Sutter in his quiet, German-accented English. "Is the Indians warfaring again?"

Marshall carefully opened his small bag and emptied its contents on a desk. Sutter leaped over to it, his eyes lighting up. "Looks like that is gold, Mr. Marshall. Where did it come from?"

"From the tailrace of the mill. There's more there. Lots more."

The ranch owner put his plump finger against his nose thoughtfully. "Now, how can we find out—ah, I know." He went to a bookcase and took out a small encyclopedia. "Here we have it. Yes, I can try it out."

He pored over the book for some time, reading the rules given for testing gold to find out if it was pure or mixed with other metals. Then he sent Marshall out to get silver coins from anybody who had them in the fort. With about three and a half dollars in silver balanced in a pair of small scales, they figured it out. This was pure gold, unmixed with silver or copper!

John Sutter sat in his big chair for a long time and stared across at his silent millwright. Gold! The word was like magic. How much would the river, and perhaps all his land, contain? Down under those waving fields of grain, those pastures where his horses and cattle and sheep grazed by the thousand—was there pure gold? What would this do to his little kingdom, where he ruled like a lord? He frowned and chewed his underlip. Somehow this news brought a fear of losing what he had struggled so long to gain.

"Mr. Marshall," he said quietly, "perhaps we had better not talk about this yet. Perhaps we had better think first of what to do? Let us preserve silence for a while."

Marshall nodded slowly. Here was a fortune. He had found it. It would be well to keep it secret from those who despised him and would perhaps steal it from him.

He went to saddle his horse. As he rode into the foothills, the sun spread across the windblown fields of grass and turned them all to shining, gleaming gold. A golden earth! Golden streams! A golden land! It should be his. Hadn't he found it?

2

Bad Medicine

Two months later John Sutter was still wondering what to do, and James Marshall, up on the American River, still kept his secret to himself. But the men who worked for him did not. Peter Wimmer spoke of it when he visited Sam Brannan's store at Sutter's Fort, and the men from the mill talked of it too. Nobody paid much attention at first, but that word *gold* was like a little bright spark in the underbrush, first a small flame here, then a tiny blaze there, no larger than the glow of a firefly. But like a fire in the brush it was active, alive, glowing, burning.

Down in the Mexican village newly named San Francisco by proclamation of the American alcalde (whose duties were somewhat like those of a mayor and judge), the spark fell. Big, roaring Sam Brannan, owner of the store, took a trip into the back country, panned out some gold, and then walked through the street telling everybody: "Gold has been found on the Rio de los Americanos. Up at Sutter's Mill—gold! Real gold!"

E. C. Kemble, editor of the California *Star*, a small weekly paper in San Francisco, heard of it but only laughed. Then he heard more, and didn't laugh. Finally he got together with two friends. Soon the three were aboard the little sloop used by Sutter to carry hides and lumber from his rancho to the town. It took them seven days to make the trip up the Sacramento River on the *Amelia*. When they stepped off at the river landing, called the *embarcadero*, an Indian took to his heels at the sight of them.

"What's the matter with that Indian?" asked Kemble. "Is he afraid of us?"

The captain of the *Amelia* laughed. "He works for Sutter. He's gone to announce our arrival. Just wait."

In a very short time the Indian returned, accompanied by a Mexican cowboy who politely presented saddled horses for their ride to the fort. As the visitors entered the fort they were greeted by its owner.

John Sutter enjoyed to the utmost his part as host. He never tired of showing hospitality to visitors who came to New Helvetia. He had given this name to his estate in honor of Switzerland, the country from which his family had come.

As John Sutter seated the three men at a long table and clapped his hands for the Indian women to bring beef and frijoles, Editor Kemble spoke.

"Captain Sutter," he said, "San Francisco is full of strange tales of gold dug up at your mill site. Is this true?"

The middle-aged Swiss pursed his lips and frowned, then he shrugged slightly and smiled.

"*Ja*, my friends. My carpenter has found some little pieces of the gold. But I do not know how much there is in the stream. Perhaps not so much. If you would like to go see, we will go tomorrow morning. So?"

"Thank you, Captain. We *would* like to see this. I don't believe that the gold find amounts to anything much. But there is a lot of talk going around the town. I want to print a true account. If it will not trouble you, we will go."

As they rode off the next day, the men politely held their horses to the gait of the slow mule ridden by the stout owner. During the journey, one of Kemble's friends asked, "Captain Sutter, how many men do you employ on this vast rancho of yours?"

"Ah, it is hard to say, my friend." Sutter's blue eyes crinkled in a smile. "Sometimes I do not know myself. But I think, right now, it is about two hundred. When we harvest grain we have nearly five hundred. All the time I have the blacksmiths, tanners, weavers, gardeners, hunters, trappers, and carpenters, as well as the vaqueros and sheepherders. You know, I brought from the Sandwich Islands some Hawaiians, and the others are Mexicans, Indians, and Americans."

"Do you thresh your grain as well, Captain Sutter?"

The fat captain laughed. "We do everything here. You should see the threshing. Grain is piled up for a month, in a mountainous pile. Then wild horses are turned loose into it, inside a corral, by the Indians, with shoutings and yelling. In an hour two thousand bushels of wheat are threshed. Some ways of the *Californios* are the best, my friends, and the quickest."

When they arrived at the American River they found the stream in flood, the mill idle, and the men unable to work. Marshall greeted the visitors with a scowl, but Captain Sutter said pleasantly, "These gentlemen have come to see the gold mines, Mr. Marshall."

The millwright did not so much as say "Howdy," for he was angry that the news had leaked out and his secret had not been kept.

"Where do we find the gold, Mr. Marshall?" asked the editor in a friendly way.

Marshall's reply was gruff. "You'll find it anywhere you've a mind to dig for it."

The three men looked at each other and then, with a shrug, wandered off to the tailrace. After an hour or so they gave up. Only one visitor had found any of the golden "color" at all, and he had but a few flakes.

It was rapidly growing dark in the mountains, and the men from the coast were startled to see Coloma Indians appearing by twos and threes. They had come to greet John Sutter, as they always did when he paid a visit to their part of the country.

The Indians squatted just outside the circle of firelight. And then, quite suddenly, their ancient chief rose and came close to the flames. He spoke with dignity, in halting Spanish.

"You look for the heavy yellow rock? My fathers knew. They saw it in the earth, in the rivers. You are my friend, Captain Sutter. I tell you, not good. That yellow earth, not good. It belongs to the great demon of the mountains. All who look for it will be eaten by the great demon."

"Where does this great demon live?" asked one of the visitors.

"In a lake of gold, far in the mountains," the chief replied. "He who tries to go there never returns. Do not look for his yellow earth. It is bad medicine."

Next morning Sutter and his guests went back to Sutter's New Helvetia, and the San Franciscans boarded the sloop for the trip back down the river. As soon as he returned, Editor Kemble printed in his paper a formal announcement of the discovery of gold. He added an account of his visit to the mill and said that, although gold was undoubtedly there, the discovery couldn't amount to much. He ended with a half column of advice "to farmers, mechanics, and all who are plying their trade successfully to stick to their calling and let the gold mines severely alone."

But now the little golden flame was merrily crackling in everybody's talk. It blazed through the small towns and villages of the California country. Gold! Gold found on the Rio de los Americanos. You can pick it up with your hands. Gold, gold, gold! The flame spread to the ships in port, to the trappers and the Mormon hunters who appeared at Sutter's Fort— to Oregon, where covered wagons were going to find good land.

Then the fire burst forth to the entire world. Gold in California! Gold! Riches and wealth! Fame and fortune! Adventure and excitement and untold treasure! That's what that one word meant to Americans, Chileans, Chinese, Dutch, English, French, Greeks—everybody. Gold!

3
The Devil's Blowhole

In Monterey during the latter part of May, 1848, the American alcalde, Walter Colton, of the United States Navy, listened smilingly to talk of gold found on the American River. The sleepy little Mexican town ninety miles below San Francisco listened, too, but joked about it.

"Ah," laughed a Spaniard to his señorita, "they say

gold has been found on the American Fork. But then they say also that a white raven was seen playing with the infant of Señor Martinez. They say that it was an owl that rang the bells of the church two nights ago! They say—but what do they not say?"

Then a stranger came into Monterey and showed about the plaza a piece of yellow ore weighing about an ounce. Old Señor Roderiguez ran for his big spyglass to look at it. Some wanted to smell it, and some to hammer it. The priest suggested melting it. An old gentleman placed it on top of his gold-headed cane and cried out, "Señores, what this stranger has brought is true gold! I challenge anyone to detect a difference." But most people didn't believe it.

The stranger left the plaza, bought supplies, and took his gold away with him. But the alcalde thought about it, and wondered. Then he sent one of his men to the distant "mines," which were not of course real mines, to find out. Word spread through the little town. A crowd assembled in the plaza to greet the alcalde's messenger when he returned. As he pulled several lumps of gold out of a buckskin bag and the people passed them about with eager fingers, all doubt was gone.

Next day the town was half deserted. Walter Colton was now alcalde for a community of women and children and the few men who were too old to walk or ride. The blacksmith put down his hammer, the farmer dropped his sickle, the baker left his bread dough, and sailors deserted their ships.

The one boardinghouse in Monterey was kept by a Yankee woman. She packed up a wagon and departed with such speed that she forgot to collect her rents. In the jail only two prisoners were left, and they began making plans to escape at the first opportunity.

The alcalde watched and wondered. He was forced to chop his own wood, draw his own water from the well, and cook his own meals, for all his servants had disappeared. Soon the alcalde found that he could stand it no longer. He would go to the mines and see what was going on. "After all," he thought, "I should send in a report to my government."

Next morning as he went out to saddle his horse he saw a Scotsman staggering down the street as if he were ill. Colton went up to the poor fellow and asked, "Is anything wrong, my friend? Have you caught the swamp fever?"

The Scotsman straightened up. "Nay, 'tis not the swamp fever. Nay, not so. 'Tis a fellow I saw at the tavern about a half hour ago. He had a lump of gold as big as me fist. Seeing it, and it not mine—why, it has given me the colic."

He staggered on down the street and went out of sight around the corner. Colton stood amazed, and then began to laugh. He hastened his packing, loading a wagon with provisions and tools. His friends Captain Marcy, Mr. Botts, and Mr. Wilkinson were going with him. To the wagon they hitched four mules, which the alcalde thought of no great power, since they were balky and not used to harness. However, they were the best he could get at the time.

The journey was not difficult to the old pueblo of San Jose, where a mission was situated. As the party left San Jose and moved toward the hills beyond the San Joaquin River, they paused to watch a herd of wild horses thundering by. The travelers held on to the halters of their own horses and mules, fearing that they would run with the herd. But the wild horses stampeded past, and the little procession wound its way into the hills, into wilder and wilder country.

On one of the paths they met a group of men who looked starved. When the men saw the party from Monterey, the whole crew ran to them, begging for food. Colton stopped at once, got out food, and passed it to them. When these dirty, ragged men had eaten, they drew from the bags slung over their shoulders enough gold to dazzle the newcomers. There must have been several thousand dollars' worth. The men wanted to pay for the food in gold, but Colton refused to take it. As they went on, and the miners continued toward the river, he shook his head in astonishment. With all that gold they had been hungry, and dressed in rags!

At last the alcalde's party came into gold country and made camp near a group of miners working in a ravine. The men were doing placer mining, with simple wooden bowls, and were taking out at the end of each day several ounces in dust or fine seedlike pieces. Colton, not wanting to get down into the mud of the ravine, got his crowbar and began to split the slate rocks. He found in the cracks particles of gold which looked like gleaming fish scales.

After several days the party moved on and went down to a plain. Here they saw a strange encampment and, on approaching it, found it to be Indian. As they came up to the camp a white man walked from a cabin and greeted them sociably.

"My name's Murphy," he said. "Will you light and eat with me?"

They sat down under the trees and Murphy called to a tall Indian woman to bring them food. "That's my wife," he explained. "She's the chief's daughter. And these other Indians dig gold for me."

"Do you pay them anything for it?" asked the alcalde from Monterey.

Murphy shrugged. "They get their food and blankets. I kill two bullocks a day for them. They are getting fat and seem contented. I've had no trouble with the Indians because I don't allow rum in camp. A rascal brought a keg here once, but I told him he had five minutes to take it away or I would knock in the top of it. Drink's what ruins them."

Colton agreed with him on that. Most of the trouble he had in his alcalde's court was with Indians who had gotten strong drink from white men.

As they were moving on, looking for new diggings, Colton noticed a man groping among some bushes. He stopped to call, "Lost something, friend?"

The man was a sailor discharged from the ship *Savannah.* "Lost something? I'll say I have. I had just filled my tin cup with nuggets when my pick accidentally struck it and tossed it halfway across this gulch. Now I can't find it."

Colton dismounted to help him look. They found the tin cup, but no gold. As he rode away, the alcalde wondered whether poor sailor Jones would ever locate his lost gold.

A few days later, as they rode through a beautiful little ravine, Colton thought he saw something moving against the face of a cliff not far away. When he went to investigate, he saw an old Mexican busily working away at a steep bank of granite and clay. It was so hard that the Mexican had great difficulty cutting into it.

"What is this for?" asked Colton. "What do you expect to get from that cliff face?"

"Señor," the man replied, "I expect to find a pocket of gold."

"What makes you think there is any gold in there? I see no sign of it."

The old man stopped, wiped his sweaty brown forehead with the back of a horny hand, and pointed across the ravine. "Do you see that hole in the cliff opposite? Well, that's a devil's blowhole. The devil blew through it and sent his gold straight into this cliff."

Colton could scarcely hold back a smile, and went on to camp a mile away on a creek where miners were digging. The next day the old Mexican hobbled into camp with his hat full of gold. At once several miners followed him back and hammered at the cliff, but never saw a sign of gold.

When they had quit, the Mexican went quietly back and dug again into the rock. He came back with another hatful of gold. He had located another pocket. Out the miners went again, but with no results.

"That's all the gold the devil blew through his blowhole," the old Mexican told Colton. "I got it. It was for me."

When the alcalde returned to his duties at Monterey, he sent in a report to the government of the United States. Gold was there in the California hills, and in considerable quantity. But as he watched men come and go with the magic stuff, he shook his head and wondered. This was some kind of fever—a fever that was changing the face of this land almost overnight. A fever that was spreading to the world. He smiled as he remembered his friend the Scotsman. He would call it the "gold-colic."

4

Let's Go!

In Indiana somebody received a newspaper that had been printed in the tiny village of San Francisco, California. It was read until nothing remained but a few worn scraps. But everybody knew what it said. It quoted the alcalde's words: "The streams are paved with gold— the mountains swell in their golden girdle. It sparkles in the sands of the valleys—it glitters in the coronets of the steep cliffs." The local paper reprinted the article but advised people to pay no attention to such reports, as they could not be true.

Then a blacksmith in the Indiana town saw an advertisement in an eastern paper for a machine to detect gold anywhere in the ground. He sent away for it. He paid for this contraption with the money he had earned by shoeing fifty horses. After he proudly displayed it to the town, he prepared to leave for California. The other young men flocked around and most of them decided to join him.

One of them got a copy of *The Pocket Guide to California: A Sea and Land Route Book*. It had a description of the new El Dorado itself, with a chapter on gold formations in the earth. There was even a map, though it did not show much.

El Dorado is Spanish for "the golden man." When Spanish explorers first went to South America, they heard stories of an Indian chief (whom they called El Dorado) whose body was covered every morning with gold dust before he jumped into a sacred lake. Later, El Dorado became the name of a fictitious kingdom, supposedly of great wealth, located somewhere on the Amazon River. Though explorers searched and searched for this kingdom, they never found it. But El Dorado came into popular use as the name for any legendary place of great riches. And it was the fantastic story of the California "El Dorado" that drew thousands westward in 1849.

A few wagons had already traveled across the vast western country, which was called the Great American Desert. But most people had been afraid to attempt such a journey into the land that John C. Frémont had explored. Now the thought of gold made them reckless.

The blacksmith gazed in beaming joy at his wonderful "gold-finding machine." The young fellows pored over the *Pocket Guide.* They all went out and bought flannel shirts, corduroy pants, high boots, and wide-brimmed hats and started looking for a covered wagon and a good team of oxen.

The news had also spread to Charleston, South Carolina. Before a store window in that city two young men stood gaping at a display of gold-mining equipment. And right in the midst of all that wonderful outlay was a gleaming, glistening, golden brick.

"Boy, if I had me a brick like that, wouldn't I have a brick, man!" one of the young men exclaimed.

"They say you can get that much gold in no time at all out in Californy," said his friend.

"That brick's pure solid gold. That card on it says so. I never have seen the like of that, not in all my born days."

"And I'll look right smart in a red shirt like that.

What do you say, Willie? Let's go!" the second young man urged.

They went into the store, where a sign, recently painted, proclaimed that the proprietor had everything needed to get you to the gold fields. They bought maps and a copy of *The Pocket Guide to California*. Poring over it by the light of a whale-oil lamp that night, they came to the conclusion that the best way to go would be to take a ship from Charleston to Panama. From there they could cross overland to the Pacific and then get passage up the Pacific coast to California.

In the store, the proprietor counted the money he had taken in that day and grinned. That gold brick was a wonderful drawing card, all right. When he had gotten in his stock of California equipment, a brilliant idea had hit him. After dark he had found a pile of old bricks. He picked out a good one and gilded it with gold paint. Then he placed against it a sign saying that here was a brick of solid ore from California.

He sold a lot of shirts and boots and picks and pans, until somebody broke into his window one night and discovered the fraud. But by that time the two young men were far out to sea, sailing toward Panama and the land of El Dorado.

In New York a middle-aged man walked down Fulton Street with a *Pocket Guide to California* clutched in his hand. He had failed in business, and to get started again he needed a lot of money in a hurry. California was a long way off, months by ship or by wagon. Suddenly he caught sight of a sign over an office. It said: WE WILL TRANSPORT YOU TO CALIFORNIA BY AIR. The man's mouth dropped open. He read the sign again and walked in.

"What does this sign mean? You can send me to the gold fields by air?"

The clerk looked up and replied, "Yes, sir, we can. Mr. Rufus Porter has designed an airship to take passengers to California."

"You mean to fly me through the air? How?"

"By means of a big balloon filled with hydrogen, propelled by six light boilers and two steam engines," said the clerk. "Do you wish to put your name on the list?"

The man went home, and after a talk with his wife, decided he would be better off looking for another job right there in New York. Later he heard that more adventurous souls did pay passage on the aircraft. But it was never finished, for lack of money. After all, who could really believe that anyone could be transported to California through the air?

But more practical plans were under way in New England. There in all the cities, the towns, and the villages staid down-easters talked of nothing but the golden opportunities in California.

"Did you hear about Lieutenant Beal, who came from California with a lump of gold? He stood on the steps of the Wall Street Stock Exchange in New York and waved the gold nugget in the face of the crowd. Then Barnum exhibited it along with Tom Thumb and the elephant. Now people are looking at it in England."

The New Englanders were very practical. Those who had money and could not go to the gold fields decided to finance those who had no money, but could go. Companies were formed, and the gold diggers agreed to share the proceeds of their labor with those who had given them money.

The best way for these seafaring New Englanders to travel would be around Cape Horn at the southern tip of South America. Then they would sail up the west coast of South America and on to San Francisco. This trip would take months, but there would be no hardship, they thought: no fevers, as in Panama; and no deserts to traverse, as across the western lands. Every old tub that could be fitted out was manned with eager sailors, and passengers were fixed up with improvised bunks in the hold.

Men swarmed on board, loaded down with red flannel shirts, high boots, wide hats, corduroy pants, picks, washbowls, and shovels. Some had odd-looking gold machines on their shoulders. Many had copies of

The Pocket Guide to California under their arms. But all had guns or pistols or both. And all had high dreams of riches.

The miners, whether they were heading for Cape Horn, the jungles of Panama, or the blistering plains, sang a song written not long before by Stephen Foster. But they made up their own words to it.

Oh! Susanna, now don't you cry for me,
For I'm off to Sacramento,
With a washbowl on my knee!

The gold fever continued to spread wildly. A clipper ship dropped anchor in the harbor of Valparaíso on the west coast of South America, and sailors went ashore.

"Where are you coming from, señores?" asked the South Americans. "California? You say there is gold on the ground in this California?" A little knot of men gathered, waving their hands, shouting excitedly. "How can we get there, to this California?"

On the other side of the Pacific Ocean an old, dirty, barnacle-encrusted tramp ship sailed into the wide bay at Sydney, Australia. A sailor displayed a nugget of gold as big as a walnut.

Men gathered around him. "What is it? Gold! Ye don't say? In California?"

The sailor leaned forward and spat on the ground. "Look, me friends. This is gold, real gold. From California." The men around the fellow with the nugget in his palm were rough and tough looking. They were ex-convicts exiled to Australia from England.

Lying on the swell of the waters of Shanghai, China, were two ships. One of them was a Nantucket whaler, and the other was a brigantine that had put in at San Francisco.

Sailors rowed to shore and gathered together. The whalers had been out nearly two years. They asked for news. The men from the other ship gave them news, but not about New England. "We stopped in California. They say there's millions in gold just lying around for anybody to pick up. I'm going back. I'll get me a million."

A curious Chinese who had learned English moved closer. He listened eagerly. Then he went out to repeat the news in Chinese. His eyes glistened and his long braid of black hair bobbed up and down as he nodded. A quick fortune might be made in this California and brought back to China. Riches! Gold!

The news spread to Europe. It traveled by mouth and in print from London to Paris, to Vienna, to Rome, to Turkey. No one had ever heard of this strange place called California. There were no maps of it to be had in Europe, but men started out anyway. They booked passage on ships that were going west. Germans, Dutch, French, Spanish! Everybody wanted gold. Some wanted adventure, too. Some wanted to get away from a dreary job, and some wanted to leave home. The talk grew wilder. There was gold out there by the bucketful! You could just kick it around with your feet!

5

Rounding the Horn

It was January, 1849, just about a year since James Marshall, the millwright, had picked up a few little pieces of gold in faraway California. Dusk was settling down over the icy waters of Boston Harbor as a sailing vessel, the *Edward Everett*, swung away from the wharf and moved to an anchorage for the night.

The decks of the tight little ship were crowded with

shouting, singing, excited gold hunters, off on the big adventure. But before the *Edward Everett* sailed, a cold wind banged chunks of ice against its bow as the men swarmed down the companionway to the cabins. The ship had been chartered by one of the many groups of men going out on a cooperative mining venture. They were university graduates, mechanics, ex-sailors, farmers—men from every kind of life—and the ship held a hundred and fifty of them.

At dawn next day, as the ship stood out to sea with the tide, a northeaster hit hard, and most of the travelers stayed in their bunks. For days Willard Farwell, the secretary of the party, was scarcely able to raise his head. When at last they reached the Gulf Stream, he got up on his shaky legs and went on deck.

Farwell had to laugh as he looked around. The old sailors of the party looked hale and hearty, but the landlubbers on board were creeping about as he was, pale and weak. As the last of them came up from below, Farwell had some ideas.

"Now that we are able to get about, why not organize a social committee? Those who can play will give us entertainment." He looked about at the various kinds of musical instruments. "And some of us can get together a weekly paper, giving the news of the ship."

So a boy of seventeen got his banjo, a bearded man swung his fiddle up to his arm, another played on his harmonica. The others joined in and sang heartily.

At the first meeting of the newspaper staff, Farwell was elected editor, and after that he went about collecting news and writing it out by hand. They could have only one copy without a press, but the reading of *The Gold Hunters' Log* on Sunday afternoon was the big event of the week. It solemnly recorded news, day by day. Once it told about a school of porpoises that had followed the *Edward Everett*. Another time the *Log* reported the rescue of young Johnny, who fell overboard while trying to haul in a bucket of water to wash his shirt.

When they neared the latitude of the Madeira Islands the wind died, and the *Edward Everett* drifted into the Sargasso Sea. There the ship could get barely enough breeze to keep its sails from slatting against its spars. On the smooth surface of the sea, Farwell saw great mats of seaweed drifting slowly. There was constant talk of the gold mines among the passengers.

"What's Californy like, you reckon? Is it hot out there, or cold? How much you think we can pan out in one day? They say—"

"I'm going to make my pile and go home to Maine to marry Jennie."

"I'll make my pile in six months. Well—it might take a year."

And here they drifted, with not enough wind to dry a wet thumb!

Then the wind came up, but from another direction. The *Edward Everett* ran down the Gulf Stream. It bowled along south to the equator, making old sea dogs of every landlubber. Then it ran into another calm for a few days, when its sail lay flat against the masts. But over there against the horizon the crew spied another ship becalmed. In great excitement a boat was lowered and some of the passengers went over to call.

This ship turned out to be another California-bound vessel, the *Aurora* from Nantucket. The ship was so old and worm-eaten a whaler that the men from the *Edward Everett* came back thankful for their tight little ship and its skillful captain.

They shook their heads, talking of it. "That *Aurora*, she'll never make it to the gold fields. She won't get around the Horn, that's a certainty!"

Just south of the equator the *Edward Everett* caught the trade winds again, and off the ship skipped, with foam against its prow.

On the thirteenth of March the wind abruptly shifted, and they struck a gale. The glass fell rapidly, and the skipper, with his eye to windward, held the ship steady on its course. The *Edward Everett* was tearing through the seas, with waves breaking over its decks. Ahead of it was the fearful rounding of stormy Cape Horn. Suddenly its foresail burst with a noise like a cannon shell, and tore away in strips.

Before they had quite recovered from that, they heard a shout.

"Fire!" yelled the cook, bounding up the companionway. "The galley's on fire!"

Farwell plunged forward, grasped a bucket in his stiff hands, and sloshed it full in a wave that washed over the rail. He was followed by several other men, who moved as best they could to the galley roof and threw the sea water down on it. The fire smoked a little and went out, but the cook was yelling loudly.

"Ye's ruined me soup! Ye'll eat salt water for your rations."

But there wasn't even time to laugh, for the ship was plunging into high seas, and sailors were moving fast, stripping its sails, making ready for the rounding of the stormy Cape. Everybody took a hand, jumping to attention at a shout from the mate. Just before darkness came, Farwell caught a brief glimpse of the land of Tierra del Fuego to the southwest, the first land the company had seen since leaving Boston.

A long, heavy swell from the Pacific Ocean came rolling in at them, a wall of gray angry water. Farwell clutched the nearest mast and held on for his life. But the little ship rose to meet its enemy. Up and up it went, and then into a deep plunge. Farwell was swung around until his arms cracked.

By the next day the ship had been blown a hundred miles to the east off its course. For weeks the ship struggled against powerful storms, and for weeks Captain Henry Smith and his crew scarcely seemed to rest or even to eat. The noise was so great—pounding, creaking, roaring of winds in hurricane fury—that Farwell felt deafened.

And then the seas grew smaller, waves were longer, the wind subsided. One day, as Farwell struggled up on deck, he saw an albatross soaring just off the stern rail. And as it turned slowly, shifting its strong wings, and planed off into the wind, a little Cape pigeon flew down and stood on the deck for a few moments. Farwell smiled a welcome to it and moved a little closer to see this tiny bird, known to all sailors who sail around the Horn. He knew that these were good signs, that the worst of the voyage was over.

In April they dropped anchor in the harbor of Valparaíso in Chile. Alongside their ship were several others on the way to the gold mines. The passengers of the *Edward Everett* sought out the last to arrive, the *Montreal,* for it was from Boston and had a touch of home.

On the fifth of June they crossed the equator on

their way north, and soon after that the whole company planned a big Fourth of July celebration. This would mark the close of the voyage, for they expected to enter the Golden Gate at San Francisco soon after. *The Gold Hunters' Log* was filled with news of the plans for the event. When the day came, the ship was sailing under a good breeze up the coast of California. Mr. Louis Lull delivered an impassioned address on the glories of the United States, not failing to mention the golden territory of California. And the Reverend Joseph Benton read aloud a poem he had written for the occasion.

Two days later the *Edward Everett* sailed into the harbor of San Francisco. The men made such a rush to the rail that it seemed to Farwell for a moment as if the ship might tip them all into the sea. But having held up under the storms of the Horn, the ship now was able to hold up under the excitement of the gold hunters.

The *Edward Everett* nosed in among the vessels crowding the bay and had some trouble docking at Clark's Point without ramming another craft. The water was so covered with ships that they bumped and scraped together at anchor.

Before the dazzled eyes of the gold hunters the small village of hodgepodge adobe houses, with tents scattered in between, was spread out in the sunlight. To them it looked like the country at the end of the rainbow—with a pot of gold waiting for every man.

6

San Francisco

As the gold rush got under way, San Francisco, until then a peaceful little village, within a few months became the talk of the world. The people of every kind and description who poured into the place had to bring tents, build shacks, or sleep on the ground under blankets draped over poles. There was no law, no organized city government that could deal with the crowds.

Men leaped from ships, fired with the urge to get into the gold fields and make their fortunes. They came by the thousands.

And then there were the miners who had dug gold and had come back to San Francisco to spend it. There was a wild gambling excitement in the air all the time.

When the *Edward Everett* docked, a young clerk-turned-gold-hunter jumped ashore with his duffel bag on his shoulders. So much equipment was strapped around him that he could hardly walk. With him was another New Englander, the first officer of the ship, who now thought he would try some prospecting.

The two walked slowly through the little town. It was about as different from their New England as anything could possibly be.

As they walked they turned to look back at the harbor. Ships were everywhere, some abandoned and at the mercy of the waves and wind. Old square-riggers were left to rot in the mud; newer vessels swung at anchor; some were hauled up on the beach and made into saloons. The *Euphemia* had been bought by the town and converted into its first jail. The *Apollo* was used as a lodging house, and the *Niantic*, stripped of its masts and rigging, was shored up at the corner of Sansome and Clay streets and taken over as a storage warehouse.

"Look at that," called the sailor from the *Edward Everett* as he pointed to a dirty old tub rolling into the jammed-up harbor. "That's the *Aurora*. The hull we said couldn't round the Horn." The boat's decks were aswarm with miners, all raring to get ashore and into the diggings.

This little town of adobe houses had every speck of ground in between the dwellings covered with tents. The two young New Englanders strolled about. Once they stopped to watch a crowd of bearded miners around a "thimble-rigger," and to see this swindler trick the audience into losing their gold. The man placed a pea under one of three small thimble-shaped cups on a barrel top. Then, as he moved the cups about, he took bets on which cup the pea would be found under. His hand was so quick and clever that gold dust seemed to move into his pouch almost as fast as the little pea moved from thimble to thimble.

"They say in the first six months of this year fifteen thousand men came here," said the clerk from the *Edward Everett*.

"Yes," his sailor friend said, "but the captain told me that on his last voyage, just after gold had been found, the town was deserted. It was like a village of the dead. Everybody ran off to the hills. The carpenter dropped his hammer. The editor closed his paper. The preacher shut up his church, and nobody remained here but a few women and children, and men too old to walk."

"Well, it looks different now. These storekeepers and gamblers must be making as much here as they would digging gold—and a lot easier for them too."

They stopped to buy a copy of the *Alta California*, a new paper started since the return of the publisher from the mines.

"You know," the sailor said slowly, "I wouldn't mind being a reporter myself. I've always had a hankering for that work. But look there at those prices!"

They stopped before a store, which had been an adobe house and was now extended out sideways by a shedlike structure, with a plank roof standing on shaky-looking posts. "Flour—forty dollars a barrel. Picks and shovels—ten dollars each. Tin pan for gold washing—butcher knife—thirty dollars."

They turned to cross the street, but stood appalled. Swampy from recent rains, the street was thick with mud. A driver urged his mules through it, yelling and howling and cracking his whip. The mud had been churned up by the wheels of ox wagons, horses, and mules. It was full of humps and holes. At one spot a horse had fallen, and four men were trying wildly to get it up. At another spot, brush and tree branches had been flung into the ruts; boxes, boards, and barrels lay on top of them.

The sailor and his friend stood watching, wondering how they could ever cross the street. Then they saw a huge miner with a heavy black beard make a flying leap onto an old piano that had settled down in the muck. "Yippee!" he bellowed as he jumped. But he was not enough of a mountain goat. One foot landed on the piano and the other went off into the mire. The piano gave way with a crack and sank deeper, and three men rushed out into the mud to haul the miner out again.

All around them the young men heard a mixture of languages: Spanish, Portuguese, English, German, French, and Swedish.

The two newcomers walked across the plaza, between the old adobe Customs House and the Parker House Hotel.

It was now time for supper. The best place seemed to be a large tent where miners were standing around waiting. Just then a Chinese gong sounded inside. At once the newcomers were almost trampled underfoot as the miners shoved through the open flap to the long tables. The meal was good, but prices were unbelievable. "Oxtail soup—one dollar; fresh eggs—one dollar each; potatoes—fifty cents; prunes—seventy-five cents."

As they left the eating place, the two would-be miners stopped to stare at a gentleman standing on the corner surrounded by a crowd. He seemed to be selling newspapers.

A young man near them said, "He's a gentleman from New York who came up from Panama on the same ship I sailed on. He had heard that reading matter is so scarce out here that anything will sell, so he brought out fifteen hundred copies of the *Tribune* from New York, and just see that! He's selling them as fast as he can pick them up at a dollar apiece."

A sudden gleam lit up his eyes. The young man turned and dashed into the Parker House Hotel. After a few minutes he emerged with some newspapers under his arm, saying, "I found a dozen papers that I had used to fill in my trunks."

"You want to sell them to me, Mister?" asked a newspaper dealer nearby. "I'll give you ten dollars for the lot."

The young man shrugged and agreed, saying, "Well, that's a gain of just about four thousand percent." He laughed and went off.

As the two young men from New England wandered through the streets they discussed plans and decided that it was not possible to stay here, where prices were so high.

They looked around for lodging houses. It took them a long time to see anything but gambling places. Tents and rough board buildings rang with the shouting and shooting of the miners. Inside by the light of whale-oil lamps, men gathered to play roulette, monte, and poker.

At last the two friends came to a rooming house. It was a rough shanty, flung together hastily near the edge of the community.

The newcomers rolled up in their blankets on the floor, but were glad when the dawn came and they could get out into the early morning light. All over San Francisco men were rising, stretching cramped muscles after sleeping on tables, on counters, or on floors. Out they came from tents and makeshift quarters that consisted of a blanket stretched on four posts. Some even got up from the sidewalks where they had spent the night.

The two young men hurried to a store, bought their supplies of bacon, cornmeal, flour, beans, and coffee. They decided to take the first boat they could get passage on up the Sacramento River to the diggings.

As they approached the landing, they had to push and fight their way through a good-natured but boisterous crowd. The only little sloop preparing to leave was packed to the rails with miners. It looked as if it might sink at any moment. The two young men stared, but could see no way of getting on board, although they had bought their tickets.

Suddenly a fight broke out on deck. Two miners

were struggling, and others around them were yelling and hooting. Splash! Overboard went one, followed by the other. The crowd on shore roared with glee, but some hurried down to help haul in the half-drowned miners.

"Quick, get on board," whispered one of the New Englanders to his friend. They pushed their way to the end of the dock and jumped into the places just vacated by the wet miners, now staggering back to town.

"All aboard!" shouted a sailor, casting off the ropes. The sails rattled into place. Then the small craft moved slowly out into the river. After a while the two friends sat down on a pile of baggage. Around them they heard talk of the diggings, and they listened eagerly.

"I'm off for Hangtown. They say the 'color' is good up that way."

"How'd you get here—by the Horn?"

"Sure. My friends from back home in Georgia wrote they're coming by way of Panama. A lot of folks are rolling across the plains now, too."

"But the traveling is fierce that way!"

"Sure. I reckon the Panama route is the best and the quickest, if you don't catch jungle fevers. Say, did you hear of the rich strike on the Mokelumne River? I may come back and try that field, if my diggings up here ain't worth much."

The two young New Englanders slept fitfully that

night on the deck. All night they fought off mosquitoes, and listened to the howl of wolves in the forests
and the lonely cry of birds along shore. And all around
them snored miners who slept with just one thought in
their heads—they would soon pick up a fortune. They
would be the lucky ones.

7

Through the Jungle

Oh! Susanna . . . I'm off to California,
With a washbowl on my knee!

All over America, Stephen Foster's song was being played. In cities and in remote villages it was taken up and sung as men and boys prepared to go gold hunting.

In one small town in New York a young fellow

named Julius Pratt joined an organized company. The group included a doctor, a lawyer, carpenters, professors, farmers, and skilled workmen of all kinds. The town turned out to wave farewell, and the whole group went to church for a last sermon. As the train pulled out for New York City the crowd sang "Oh! Susanna."

Their little brig, the *Mayflower,* was almost lost in the vast, crowded shipping on the New York water-front. Julius stared in astonishment. Ships of every kind, taking on passengers for California, were jammed together.

The group hurried on board, for the *Mayflower* was to sail next day for the Isthmus of Panama.

Julius Pratt had brought two large bags of dimes to pay expenses as he crossed the Isthmus. He had heard that dimes were rated as *reals* there, and eight of them equaled a dollar. He also had with him a tent and all supplies for simple camp life, and had shipped further provisions to California on a vessel going around the Horn. As the *Mayflower* sailed with the tide next day, a shout broke from the decks and the men jigged and sang as if they were off to a picnic.

The captain looked at his first officer and laughed. "Just wait till we pass Sandy Hook. We won't see hide nor hair of them for a while."

Sure enough, a gale hit the *Mayflower* almost at once, and for some days the passengers were pale and sick. Julius was ill, too, and no less frightened than the others by the baggage, which had been piled carelessly amidship and not stowed away. It slid back and forth with every roll and pitch of the ship, making it most dangerous to try to cross the cabin.

When the gale had subsided, Julius got himself out of his bunk and up to the deck. It took about three weeks to arrive at Chagres, on the Gulf of Mexico side of Panama. By that time the passengers had recovered their spirits and were filled with energy again.

As the party from the *Mayflower* went ashore in small native boats, they began to discuss plans for crossing the Isthmus. So many miners were going that way now that the trip up the Chagres River had become very difficult and expensive. On shore in front of the native huts, the party decided to organize as a military company for convenience and protection. Julius Pratt was elected captain because he could speak Spanish.

At once he went off to find Indians who would take them by native boat up the Chagres River to Gorgona. From there they would have to travel twenty-eight miles by mule trail.

Julius made a good bargain with an Indian, who

agreed to take them to Gorgona. It was April, and as his boat shoved off Julius could see dark green jungle growth peeping over the riverbanks. Brittle palm leaves were rustling in a small breeze from the Gulf of Mexico. As night came down abruptly over the jungle, the men from the United States strained their eyes but could see nothing. All around them the jungle was coming awake. Julius heard cries of wild beasts and the strange singsong chants of the Indians.

At about eleven that night, the would-be miners landed near several palm huts. The next morning as the party sat eating breakfast, the Indians went aside and talked in low guttural tones. Julius frowned and began to worry. One Indian approached and announced that they would go no farther. They were not getting enough money.

Julius quietly picked up his shotgun, and the other men of the party drew revolvers and trained their weapons on the crew.

"All right now," snapped Pratt. "You made an agreement to row us to Gorgona. Get in the boats."

Sullenly the Indians obeyed, but they sang no more, and the party was very glad to get ashore and see them disappear downriver when Gorgona had been reached. Here they held another council.

Gorgona was little more than a collection of huts,

and other Americans sat about complaining. Word came from Panama City that conditions there were bad, too, with hundreds of stranded Americans starving or dying of jungle fever. The party agreed with Julius that it would be better to camp here on the banks of the Chagres and go on to Panama City when word of a ship's arrival came in.

Three weeks later the rainy season began, and the mule trail promised to become a sea of deep mud. The party hired mules and Indians to lead them. Then, tying their boxes on behind, the travelers started out. When they reached Panama City they could hardly walk for the thick mud caked on their legs, and several of them were already ill with jungle fever.

Julius went out to look for a ship. In the harbor was an old hulk of a vessel called the *Humboldt*, which was anchored there as a storeship for coal. The owner refused to allow it to sail, but finally Julius persuaded him to make the ship ready for a voyage to San Francisco. The passenger list was to be limited to four hundred.

Julius and his party paid their money and went on board, only to find that already more than four hundred passengers had been taken on, many of them ill with fever. No food had been provided. All day long the men quarreled and cursed and fought. Julius got his party together, and they drew their weapons again. Marching grimly from the boat to the home of the ship's owner, they shouted:

"Come out here in the street! We want to talk to you."

The frightened owner crept slowly out and stood trembling, for other men from the ship had followed the Pratt party and were shouting and yelling behind them.

"You will remove the extra passengers from the ship and provide food for the voyage, or we will take you on board with us."

"Gentlemen, gentlemen, I agree," said the ship's owner. "I did not know that these unfortunate things had happened. It was my manager who did this to you."

But what to do with the extra passengers? At dawn another vessel sailed into the harbor, and the problem was solved. A hundred men were removed to the newly arrived ship, and provisions were brought aboard the old *Humboldt*. The following day the ship sailed, but Julius Pratt would never forget as long as he lived that terrible voyage. The water tasted poisonous, the food was almost impossible to swallow, and almost every day there was a death on board.

At Acapulco, Mexico, the Pratt party could stand

conditions on the ship no longer. They went ashore and decided to wait for another vessel. After two weeks, one of the new steamers just put into use came into port, on its way to San Francisco. Julius hurriedly sought out the captain, and found him in a café near the waterfront.

"Well, now," said the skipper, frowning. "I don't see as I can take you fellows aboard. My ship is crowded to the gunwales. I've got more passengers than the legal limit. They fight all day for what little rations they can get, and there's no place to sleep the ruffians we've got aboard now."

"We've been here two weeks, and we've got to get to California. We'll do anything to get out of here," Julius insisted.

"Well, now, I tell you," said the captain, "if you'll take sailor's rations—hardtack and salt junk—I'll take a vote amongst the passengers."

The party hastily got together and went to the ship. Here they moved about making friends with the passengers.

When the captain came on board he shouted, "Be ye willing to take on these men?"

"Why not?" shouted a big fellow. "What's the difference? We got so many we won't notice a few more."

The ship steamed away from Mexico and up the

coast to San Francisco. Seven months from the day they had left the harbor of New York, the Pratt party steamed through the Golden Gate to San Francisco. They stepped ashore on the promised land, battered, weary, and worn, but with red shirts, corduroy trousers, slouch hats, picks, pans, pistols, and all. Off to the diggings! Off to the gold mines!

8

Six-Shooter City

San Francisco was changing so rapidly that a miner who left it and then returned two months later could scarcely recognize the place. All through the strange city of tents and shacks there was a constant sound of hammering as buildings went up. Yet more and more tents were raised too, until they spread out into the low evergreen bushes and up the hillsides. Every day the harbor was becoming a greater forest of masts and spars, of ships dropping anchor, and of deserted vessels.

It was hot in San Francisco that summer. "Forty-Niners" who burst ashore from the constantly arriving ships sweated and looked for a spot out of the sun. The streets were dry; dust flew up in clouds under the feet of horses and oxen and mules.

One afternoon a man named Krafft came to the plaza. He had spent the last three days taking care, as best he could, of men sick and dying of scurvy, of dysentery, of rheumatism, of pneumonia, and of typhoid fever. He wasn't a doctor. He was just a kindly man who was trying to aid the helpless sick. At that time the town had no hospital, no doctors or nurses. There were doctors in California, but they were all knee-deep in dirt or water up at the diggings.

Mr. Krafft had become so angered by the conditions around him that he began shouting in a booming voice to anyone on the plaza who would listen:

"Your Honor and gentlemen," he shouted as if to a judge. "We are very sick, and hungry and helpless and wretched. If somebody does not do something for us we shall die. All we ask is a fair chance; and we say again, upon our honor, gentlemen, if somebody does not do something for us, we shall die!"

But nobody listened long. There was a parade coming down the street. The men on the walks pressed forward to see better. This was a crowd of tough-looking men in ponchos with Spanish serapes about their shoulders. A few even had Chinese robes thrown over their backs. They carried pistols and knives and guns, and as they passed, yelling and shouting, a cry went up:

"It's the Hounds!"

The crowd began to melt away as the paraders were recognized. This was an organized band of the toughest men in town. They called themselves the Regulators, but everybody else called them the Hounds. Pretending to "do justice," they attacked stores, gambling houses, and groups of foreigners.

"They're heading for the Chilean quarter!" someone shouted.

"Why aren't they arrested?" asked an indignant woman.

"You better get out of sight, ma'am," answered a miner, pushing her behind a barrel. "Might start off with a six-shooter any minute. They're bad actors, ma'am. Why ain't they arrested? Because this town ain't got no police force. Ain't got no courts or judges that're worth a panned-out diggin'! This town practically belongs to them Hounds."

A shot was heard, then screams, then a volley of shots in an outlying section of town. After a while the

Hounds came back, loaded now with any belongings that had appealed to them before they set fire to the little homes of the Chileans. With fife and drum and even a flag flying, they paraded up and down the town. Everybody knew that when night fell the Hounds would come out again to raid saloons, break into stores, make off with whatever they could carry, and destroy the rest.

It was nine o'clock. San Francisco seemed to be growing noisier by the hour. On the plaza a crowd gathered in front of the schoolhouse to pay three dollars for admission, then waited till the doors opened. A musician was to appear in a program of musical monologues, recitations, and imitations.

"Look, there's a lady!" Heads turned quickly. "Four of 'em, too."

As the doors opened, the group of miners became strangely orderly and quiet. They waited politely for the four ladies to enter and take reserved seats at the front. The Forty-Niners took care to spit their tobacco juice behind them, so they would not offend the ladies, and some even went so far as to remove their hats.

"Here comes the piano!" one of the crowd shouted.

Proudly borne by stalwart miners, the piano was carried into the schoolhouse. It belonged to Mr. Harrison, collector of the port. Every time it was used for a concert it had to be carried to the schoolhouse and then back to its owner's home.

As the performer charmed his audience with his birdcalls, imitations, and songs, a sound penetrated the building from outside. Miners craned their necks around, and then as they realized what the sound was, they stampeded for the door. In a few seconds the place was deserted except for the four ladies and the entertainer.

There were cries of "Fire!" "Bring the buckets!" "Fire!"

The Hounds were out again. Everybody ran to the far side of town, where a store was burning. The hoodlums had looted the place, shot at its proprietor, who was sleeping there, and then set fire to it. Men dashed wildly about dumping water on the flames with buckets filled from horse troughs and rain barrels. The plank store burned in a matter of minutes as the owner stood outside, pale and stricken. Next to it a tent blazed up, and then another. But the crowd managed to wet down the outlying areas, and in a little while the fire was out. Those who had bought tickets to the show went back to get their money's worth.

Next day a crowd of irate citizens milled around the center of town. The alcalde, stirred to action by angry citizens, had called for a meeting.

In the midst of the crowd was Sam Brannan, no

longer running a store at Sutter's Fort, but now a big man in San Francisco. Sam got up and spoke, denouncing the Hounds and asking for action. A collection was taken for those who had suffered at the hands of the thieves and hoodlums, and a volunteer police force was organized. It was made up of two hundred and fifty grim men, armed and ready.

That afternoon the leader of the Hounds and twenty of his followers were captured, and then jailed on board the United States ship, the *Warren*. The following week they were sentenced to ten years' imprisonment at hard labor. But the town was so disorganized, with jury and judge constantly disappearing into the gold fields, that the men were not punished, though several of them were sent out of the country. The others went off to the gold mines along with all the strangers pouring into California.

Out there in the diggings it was easy enough to hide out. Nobody asked who you were so long as you didn't jump any claims.

9

"Oh! Susanna!"

By 1848 the great western wilderness land of mountains, plains, and deserts was known only to the few who had ventured in wagon trains to the coasts of Oregon and California. It was still unknown country to everybody else except Indians and trappers and explorers.

Pioneer settlements had pushed beyond the Mississippi, but it had taken the pioneers two hundred and twenty years to get that far. Then the word *gold* swept the whole land, and people forgot the miles of deserts and mountains. They started by hundreds, and then went by thousands. Every route westward was choked with wagons, mules, horses, carts, wheelbarrows, and people.

Rolling and rattling and bumping and shouting came the Conestoga wagons into St. Joseph, Missouri. The rush to California was on. Some women and children came, but most of the emigrants were men. Men rode horses and drove mules. "Gee up there!" "Git along!" They yelled and shouted and swapped stories.

The air around St. Joseph was filled with excitement, and the earth was enveloped with clouds of dust. Some travelers pushed wheelbarrows filled with provisions. Men cracked their whips over teams of six or eight oxen, drawing canvas-covered wagons. "Whoa there. Haw!" Crack went the long bullwhips.

Once in a while you could see an old scout with his coonskin cap, tail dangling on his neck, spitting tobacco and moving quietly about in buckskin clothes.

At a campsite just outside St. Joseph, smoke rose from countless fires, and the smell of corn pone and bacon filled the air. The people gathered there were mostly decent, respectable folk. They were ready to help one another when needed.

"Look, Pa, we can't start tomorrow," a boy would call. "Our left rear axle is busted almost through. Must have been that time we went in the gully." At once several men would leave their own wagons and come to help with axe and hammer and great good will.

One day a hundred wagons came into the camp to spend the night on a sandbar in the Indian nation over the river from St. Joe. The travelers sat around the campfires singing "Home, Sweet Home" and "Life on the Ocean Wave."

But clouds came up during the night and the campers awoke to a gray, wet sky. James Abbey, a young man from New Albany, Indiana, felt the cold rain beating on his face and thought longingly of his home, his mother, and his dry and comfortable bed. He was soaked, but a cup of coffee that his friend Billy managed to make in the rain warmed him and set him to thinking of the adventure ahead. The long line of wagons formed. "Everybody ready? Let's go."

Somebody struck up a tune on a fiddle. Somebody else began to sing, and one, then another joined in. Soon the whole line had taken up the song:

"Oh! Susanna, now don't you cry for me,
For I'm off to California,
With a washbowl on my knee!"

The first day seemed long. At a small creek they found the shores so steep and muddy that they could hardly get down to the stream, where a ford had been filled in with brush cut by earlier travelers. The first wagons got across all right, then one, more heavily loaded, sank in the mud to the axle and had to be hauled out by all hands.

That afternoon, as Jim Abbey walked alongside his wagon on a flat grassy prairie, his dog barked sharply. Then a horse shied. Jim reached for his gun as he heard a sound. He fired, and killed a big rattlesnake. During that day he and his friends shot seven other snakes. After that the men kept a close watch.

As they rolled on, Jim was amazed to see along the trail all sorts of objects thrown away by their owners. There was a handsome chest, and over there were a couple of barrels of molasses. Jim reached down once and picked up a *Guide to the Gold Fields*. Was that a cooking stove? Somebody had started with it, then found it easier to cook on open fires made of dried buffalo chips, as the other emigrants did.

One evening a large herd of buffalo came so close that the old scout with the party warned them, "Watch out sharp for a stampede, boys. Them buffalo can flatten this camp in no time a-tall." The men stood about watching with anxious eyes as the herd moved along. Then some of the men rode out to kill a stray buffalo and brought welcome fresh meat to camp that night. But the buffalo gnats were so bad that Jim thought his very ears were on fire, and the horses and oxen were driven nearly frantic.

Sometimes Jim had to laugh as he read the wagon names: "Rough and Ready," "California by Thunder," and "Sacramento or Bust." But most of them had "The Elephant" painted on the canvas. "Seeing the Elephant" was a way of saying "I'm going to see everything." Back in New York, P.T. Barnum's best attraction was an elephant. It was the last thing to be seen in his show, and the most wonderful. Now the people began to talk of the worst part of the trip as "The Elephant."

In June the wagon party was two months away from home in Indiana. The long trains had split up, finding that fewer wagons traveling together were just as safe from Indians, and more convenient. Jim's wagon was with a train of seven, with an elected captain in charge.

Now they were passing many graves along the trail. Jim was thankful that all members of his train were well, for cholera was bringing sudden death to many men, women, and children on the trail. They still had enough grass for their stock, since this had been an unusually good year for grass on the great plains. But water was often so poisonous that it was dangerous for man or beast. Fuel was scarce, too, and sometimes they had to gather dried grass to cook a meal, or had to eat their bacon raw.

They were ferried across the Platte River at Fort Laramie, and entered a different kind of country. Here the earth was filled with alkali, salt, and sulfur, and all along the way they saw skeletons of horses, mules, and oxen. Jim's ox team had sore feet, but nevertheless they plodded along.

The travelers saw the mountains looming ahead, and came to the Sweetwater River, where animals and humans could not seem to drink enough of the pure stream. Then they traveled on over rough, rocky roads until they reached the Great Divide, where Pacific Spring sent its waters toward the Pacific Ocean.

Some trains took a route called Sublette's Cutoff. The others went on to Salt Lake City, where the Mormon colony had recently ended its long trek from Nauvoo, Illinois. Jim's train went to Salt Lake, and then headed for California.

"Look at that," called Jim as they entered the desert country. All around them were dead animals and human graves. It was a horrible place, with no grass for the oxen and nothing in sight but prickly pear and sage. The men walked, to save their stock, their lips parched and their tongues swollen. At night it was cold, and the change from the burning heat of day to freezing temperatures at night gave many of the emigrants colds that changed quickly to pneumonia.

"What will all those animals behind us do, with the grass giving out like this?" Jim asked the old scout. The only answer the old-timer could give him was, "Die, I reckon."

Now they had another hazard. By day they met Indians, who seemed friendly. They had picked up a few expressions from listening to the drivers, and greeted them with "Whoa, haw. How de do!" But at night raiding parties came in under cover of darkness and stole horses or shot arrows into oxen.

One day the travelers came upon a party burying a man who had been shot by an Indian as he stood guard the previous night. Then they passed the Humboldt Sink and crossed a short desert. Jim counted the cast-off wagons, but when he got to three hundred and sixty-two he quit. It made him dizzy.

"I reckon we've passed 'The Elephant' right here," he said to his friend Billy as they crossed the hot sands.

But they hadn't. "The Elephant" was to be the crossing of the Sierra Nevada mountains. It wasn't far to the gold fields now, just beyond the range of snow-covered peaks ahead of them.

Then they began to climb. Men were tired, and oxen and horses almost done in. But they climbed up and up.

Descending the mountains on the far side was not much easier, as it took great care and labor to keep the wagons from running headlong into the canyons. But at last they saw below them the valley, where flowers bloomed and cold, rushing streams bore golden promise. This was the promised land—California.

Jim drew a deep breath of the sweet air, fragrant with pine and spruce, and his weary muscles seemed to revive. Down they went, slowly, but toward the end of the journey.

They had left in April. It was now August. As the wagons rattled into the mining camp of Weaverville, nobody looked up to welcome them. There were too many new people coming in all the time. But Jim felt that California itself welcomed them. He hitched up his pants, grinned at Billy, and cried, "Come on, fellow, let's go. Where's my pick and pan? Where's the gold?"

10

Shovel and Pan

Where was the gold? The boys talked of it that night around their fire. Old-timers drifted by and told them what they knew. The gold was in the earth and streams, in what was called the mother lode. This was a layer of gold-veined quartz rock running for many miles through the bedrock of the mountains and hills of the Sierras.

Placer gold was gold that had broken away from quartz outcroppings by the action of rain and snow and falling water. It had washed down into the streams and had been left in the powdered dirt of dry gulches.

Jim Abbey spent a restless night dreaming of a golden fortune. Next morning he and Billy were advised by an old prospector to auction off their stuff. Accordingly they held an auction and promptly sold the wagons, oxen, and what goods they had left. Then the money was divided and the boys were on their own.

Jim and Billy, who had now been joined by another companion named Rowley, decided to work together for a while. Jim bought a pointed shovel for thirteen dollars and a pick for four dollars and fifty cents. Their pans and buckets they had brought with them. The pans could be used for washing out gold or frying flapjacks. They were also useful for frying miner's bread, which was a mixture of flour, water, and saleratus for rising.

"This work ought to be easy for us, Jim," said Billy as they walked out of Weaverville and into the hills. "We're so toughened by overland travel, this digging will be nothing."

After a time the trail led them near several bearded miners working in a gulch. The boys decided to try their luck nearby. At first they dug so fast and hard that the earth and rocks flew into the air, and the other miners who had had more experience laughed at them, calling out: "Hold your fire, me boys. 'Tis tuckered out ye'll be in two shakes of a mule's tail."

But the boys dug their pointed shovels into the rich earth as if they expected a treasure to come up with every shovelful. Then they filled their pans with loose earth and sand and shook them back and forth, sending the larger portion of dirt over the sides. With the pans full of dirt they clambered down to a small stream, where other miners were busy washing for gold. They filled a pan with water, sloshed it back and forth, and carefully washed out the sand. Two of the pans held nothing, but in his pan Jim saw a few little particles lying heavily at the bottom. They were a dark color, not much like gold, but he knew that he had found something.

"Yippee!" he yelled, bringing his two friends loping over to him. "I've found it. Gold!"

A couple of the other miners came to see. One said, "Yep, that's the color. It's about four dollars' worth."

All day they dug and washed and searched, but with no further reward. That night Jim and his friends could hardly move to cook bacon and fry some bread. Their muscles ached as if they were on fire.

"Did somebody say we were tough after crossing the

plains and deserts and the Sierra Nevada?" Jim groaned. "I might as well be right from the city, with muscles like cheese."

"That's right," answered Billy, easing his long body carefully back on the earth and looking up at the brilliant stars. "This work sure does bend a man down. Just shaking that pan hurts me all over."

But California was fine country. The air was wonderful and there was no rain from spring till fall. The days were so warm that the boys felt like shedding their flannel shirts as they worked, but the nights were chill and they were glad to have their warm blankets. They had a tent, but used it to keep their gear in, preferring to sleep under the stars with the pines and firs scenting the air.

Next day their diggings gave out and they went looking for a new claim. But every spot of ground appeared to be pitted with holes and filled with men. Next night Jim wrote in his diary that they had washed out fifty buckets of dirt and got about a half ounce of gold, wet feet, and aching bones.

Then that hole gave out. "Come on, boys, let's search for new claims," he called, and they wandered around again. "Here, this looks like a likely place to me. Let's dig here."

They set to work, laboring as hard as any poor fellows ever did, and carrying their dirt about four hundred yards over rocks to the creek. They got half an ounce. Tired out, they sat down in the shade to eat the beans that they had cooked all night in a pot in the hot ashes on their campfire. Nearby were groups of miners of all kinds and descriptions. Jim looked at them with interest. One was a man of about thirty, with a red beard that thrust out at a belligerent angle as he worked. He had a cradle, or "rocker," and there was nobody helping him.

The boys watched with interest, for they were beginning to realize that they had to have one of these contraptions to save time and effort. This man seemed to work out three times as much dirt with the rocker as the boys did with their three pans. It looked like a baby's cradle as the miner rocked it from side to side with one hand, and then stopped to shovel dirt into it with the other. It had a flat bottom with two flared-out sides, and the end was open except for a slat of wood to collect the gold that might pass another slot near the middle. At the head of the rocker was a hopper with a wire screen or a sheet-iron bottom in which there were holes. Under this was an apron or board sloping downward from the head. It was fastened on two curved wooden pieces, which allowed it to rock back and forth.

"How can we get one of them things, Jim?" asked Billy enviously. "That man told me it cost him about a hundred dollars."

"Well, the only way I know is to either make one or save up our panned gold till we get enough to buy one in Sacramento. They say rockers are made down there, and the man who makes them is getting rich hand over fist."

"All right, then let's move on and keep digging."

They went five miles farther along the creek. Down here it was so hot in the sun that they had to stop work after five hours and rest in their tent awhile. That night Jim had almost no rest, for he was too tired to sleep. As he lay awake he heard an owl hooting in the forest and wondered if the Indians out there ever went on the warpath. He heard the howl of a black wolf, too, and shivered as the sound rose and sank into silence.

The day before, a miner had told Rowley of a friend who had wandered too far away from camp at night and had been found the next day killed by the wolves. Next morning when they got up they discovered tracks around the camp so huge that they could scarcely believe their eyes. A Mexican miner camped nearby shrugged his shoulders, pulled his scarlet serape from his shoulders as the sun grew hot, and said, "That is the grizzly, amigos. A big beast, too, that señor was.

He came smelling and smelling us in the night. But he went away."

That day was the hardest they had yet spent. For hours the three dug and then shouldered bags of earth to the creek. "And," mumbled Jim, "if carrying sacks of dirt all day in the broiling sun over stones and up steep slopes isn't hard work, then I don't know what hard work is."

The day's labor produced nine dollars and a few cents for the three of them. But they decided to stay a while longer, for the fellow next to them had struck it rich. He had been digging with no luck, and then had found a pocket. In one moment he had dug up about seventy-five dollars' worth of gold!

After a while Jim got out his knife and went crevicing. Some pockets were in walls of rock and could be dug out with a butcher knife. He probed and dug and pried off pieces of rock, but found no pockets, and so went back to his panning.

"Say, boy," drawled the man resting next to him as the sun went down. "This is called Weaver Creek. You know, last year a rancher named Weber came here with about a thousand Indians. For just the grub he gave them, those Indians dug for him till he got about fifty thousand dollars. See those pits over there? That's where he was."

"Well," replied Jim despondently, "in that case we

had better move to better diggings. He must have got it all, near about."

The boys wandered around, digging a claim wherever they thought they might strike it rich and "make their pile." But their luck was never very good.

Jim got used to hard work and rough living, digging and panning and working with the new rocker they had bought. And on Sunday, when the other boys went to town, he seldom felt like going with them. Instead he thought of home and his quiet, peaceful life there, and went to sit under the trees and write letters to his mother and sister. As he wrote he raised his head to listen. The boys were singing as they plodded down the trail. Fainter and fainter the sounds came to him:

"Home, sweet, sweet home!
There's no place like home."

11

River Town

In 1849, what had been Sutter's embarcadero was a noisy, busy camp where miners bought and gambled, talked and drank. Emigrants trudging wearily into the camp, now called Sacramento, stared curiously at the tent town. Its people were too busy to grow vegetables or fruit, so a wagonload of onions and potatoes hauled from the mission of San Jose brought a dollar a pound.

Boats were moored for a mile down the river, and piled up on the banks were barrels, boxes, trunks, and bales. Several of the ships anchored there were used as storehouses. A crowd gathered, cheering and yelling, whenever a new vessel from San Francisco docked.

Two miners talked as they sat on a box and waited for the steamer *McKim* to chug up the river. A crowd was gathering, for the *McKim* was the first steamer of any size to arrive at Sacramento. Everybody was dressed up in Sunday best and in high spirits on this September day.

Down the stream from Sutter's Fort sailed a vessel, the *Eliadora,* a Chilean brig owned by Sam Brannan, who was moving his store from the fort to Sacramento. The crowd watched with interest as the vessel was warped into the dock and Indians began to carry boxes and barrels ashore.

"That's too bad for old man Sutter," said one of the miners. "His fort was the only trading post in this part of the country. Now it's about gone. Nobody there anymore. Sam Brannan knows he'll do right well here in Sacramento, even if he does spend most of his time in San Francisco."

"Here she comes. Look at her ride!" A terrific shout went up, and the people surged to the shores. "Ain't she a beauty? I'm going down on her next trip."

The little *McKim*, not so big, but yet the biggest side-wheeler to come up the river, slowly headed for the docks. On deck a big man with a booming voice bellowed out orders at the top of his lungs.

"That the captain?" asked a man on the dock.

"Naw," his friend replied. "That's the third officer, Bill Corlett. Might as well be the captain, though. He runs the ship. They say he caught two Chinamen robbing a passenger's cabin on the *Defiance*. Know what he did? He sloshed them overboard till they were spouting water like dolphins.

"He don't like gamblers neither, and they say he'll heave one overboard quick as you can sneeze, if he catches one on his ship."

"He sure ought to come ashore and start in here, then. Every other tent in this town's got a gambling table or two."

"Worse'n that. Even the grocery stores have got gambling tables, or at least the old shell game on the top of a hogshead."

"Not Huntington's store. He makes plenty of money, all right, on the prices he charges for miners' supplies."

The men got up and strolled back into the little town. Every other shack or tent seemed to be an eating place, but prices, as in San Francisco, were very high. When the miners came in with their pokes of gold they were completely reckless with their money, and they wanted excitement, good food, entertainment—at any cost.

Behind Sacramento a line of timber marked the wilderness. Grizzlies, cougars, and black wolves left tracks so close to the "city" that it was an easy matter to hunt them down. On the north side of the town was a deep swamp, where cattle continually wandered, only to sink into it and die. The smells from the slough came in when the wind was from that way. They competed with the town smells of fried meat, Mexican frijoles, garbage in the streets, and wandering horses, mules, pigs, and oxen.

The noise of hammer and saw was continuous. Shanties of logs and rough board planking went up in short order. Over there was the first theater building, just finished, boasting the name of the Eagle. It took the place of a tent, where entertainers had put on shows for some months past. Actors and musicians and dancers were listed in the papers as planning trips to the mines. They were welcomed by the Forty-Niners, who came in droves and pelted the performers with gold when the entertainment met with their loud-voiced approval.

A moody-looking young man, rather Germanic in dress, stood staring at the boisterous crowd as if in a nightmare. It was young Sutter, the eldest son of the kindly old man who had carved a little kingdom in this wilderness. Young Sutter had come over from Europe expecting to find himself the prince of his father's domain. Now he discovered that his father's fat lands and herds had shrunk to almost nothing. Sutter's Fort was about deserted.

The old man, who had tried to regain his fortune by trade and selling merchandise, had failed. People had come as squatters and taken possession of all his holdings. They had seized his embarcadero and converted it into a town almost overnight. They had started stores and drawn regular customers from the fort. They had shot the cattle and fought off with their six-shooters and pistols the few men who remained to work for Sutter. The old man could do nothing.

His claims were ignored. There was no law in the land except the law of the camps made by the miners themselves. John Sutter had withdrawn to his Hock Farm on the river, where he spent his time trying to keep a few Indians working for him. The last of his men had deserted him to hunt gold.

Now, unhappy young Sutter was trying to make his father's claims known to the government, and to figure out means of fighting off the cattle thieves and cut-throats. These lawless men hid in dense woods near Hock Farm, and ran off some of the Sutter stock every day to sell for beef in Sacramento.

Young Sutter was worried about his mother, Anna, who was coming from Europe with his younger brothers and sisters. She expected to find here the security and wealth and comfort that she had not had in Switzerland.

Once even his father had gone gold seeking, taking his Indians and Kanakas from Hawaii to dig for him. At first they worked willingly, but soon the workmen began to understand that they could dig gold for themselves. They deserted and each man started out on his own. Now John Sutter and his son felt that immediate statehood for California was the only hope for their future.

As young Sutter watched the crowd, Collis Huntington, the big merchant of the town, walked by with his wide-brimmed hat coming down almost to his shoulders. Huntington was a Connecticut Yankee, as shrewd and penny-pinching as they made them. The son of old John Sutter had heard many stories of this Huntington who had crossed the Isthmus of Panama the year before. When held up for three months at Panama, he had not hung idly around. Instead, he had chartered a small ship, loaded her up with sacks of jerked beef, potatoes, rice, and syrup, and sold them at a great profit. When other Argonauts, as the gold hunters were called, reached California with little or no money, this Yankee stepped ashore with five thousand dollars.

And he didn't rush off to dig gold, either. He put up a store, which drew the trade from Sutter's Fort and, hoarding his merchandise when prices were low, he sold his goods when prices were high. Now he had a group of young men working for him who were alert and active all day because he had a rule that they had to be in bed by nine o'clock. None of "his boys" were to be seen in gambling halls or saloons.

Huntington had a way of going down to San Francisco every so often to replenish his stock. He would stand on Clark's Point with a powerful pair of field glasses. When he saw a ship sailing in he would leap into his skiff and row out to its side. Climbing aboard, he would bargain for the cargoes, and pay a deposit on them from bags of gold fastened to a belt around his waist!

Young Sutter thought that perhaps his father should decide to sell out at the fort completely and retire to his farm for good. The place was about deserted now, anyway. It was an ironic situation. This land where the tent city stood belonged to his father and to him. But what could they do about it?

12

Miner's Holiday

The hills up from Sacramento had become dotted with little towns in the eighteen months since Marshall had seen that glint in the mill tailrace. Six days during the week the rocks rang with the clang of pick and shovel. But Sunday was different—even in Coloma, which was just a collection of tents and shacks thrown up hastily on the site of Sutter's Mill. Early in the morning Charlie Gillespie put on his best shirt, dug some of the mud from his boots, hitched up his pants, and shoved a poke of gold dust into a pocket. He was ready to join the mob of diggers for a day of recreation.

The plank sidewalks on the one main street rattled and creaked with the miners' heavy boots. Charlie rubbed elbows with a thoroughly good-natured crowd. There were Kanakas from Hawaii, Peruvians and Mexicans and Chileans in their bright serapes, black men run away from the slave states, Frenchmen, cockney English, and Germans, Dutch, and Swedes. Yankees and slow-spoken Georgians and Chinese all moved by him. He heard the chattering of dozens of languages. A few Indians stood quietly in front of the saloons.

In the dusty street were gamblers shouting, "Come try your luck at the good old shell game! See the little pea. Now you see it, now you don't. Place your bets, gents, on which shell it's under!" Miners crowded about a man who had his boot resting on a block of wood, his three little nutshells placed on his thigh, as on a table. String-game tricksters called, "Can you put your finger in the loop, gentlemen? Make your bets on it! Three, six, or eight ounces of gold on it."

There, perched on a big box before a small canvas tent, was a down-east auctioneer, selling his goods "at bargain prices." "Come and get your gear, boys," he bellowed. "Red shirts, hats, wool caps, and the best pair of boots you ever saw. Come get your mud-splashers, your road-smashers, boys."

Charlie, with his friends, moved a little closer. He needed a new pair of boots, and thought he had better get these, if they fit. He tried them on and decided they would do. His friends pushed closer, everybody offering a comment.

" 'Tain't the latest style in Paris, boy," shouted one red-bearded fellow. "You better get a pair with red tassels on 'em." Everybody roared at the joke.

"Look at the soles, Charlie. Don't get tricked with an old pair shined up," one of his friends cautioned.

The auctioneer continued his din. "Going, going, gone for four and a half ounces! Sold. Step up here, sir, and weigh out your gold dust."

Every seller had a tiny scale as part of his equipment, to weigh out his payment for merchandise. Charlie took out his dust and had it weighed. Dust was worth fourteen dollars an ounce. That was too much money for a pair of boots, but a man had to have boots to dig gold to pay for them.

Behind him a friend was buying mining supplies from a tent store. He needed a butcher knife for digging the gold out of rocks. Charlie and the others bought sugar, coffee, bacon, and beans and, with sacks of flour on their shoulders, went off to put them in a friend's tent till they were ready to leave. In an hour's time the auctioneer had sold out, packed up his gold dust and scales, and moved out of the street.

"Everybody scatter!" The cry rang down the little camp street. "Look out! It's the Troopers."

Charlie had never before seen the boys known as the Troopers, but he had heard of them. So he leaped to safety out of the street as a band of riders swept in, sending the crowd flying. Down the street they rode, yipping and yelling like Indians on the plains. These men had been in the army, fighting Indians, and could ride as well as the Indians themselves. Now they began to perform all kinds of stunts. They threw themselves from side to side on their snorting mounts, picked up hats flung on the ground, then suddenly reined in their horses just before overrunning the cheering crowd.

Charlie and his friends moved along to the dining tent, and after an expensive but satisfying meal, strolled along talking to everybody they met. In the crowd was a lawyer, now a waiter in the eating tent, and the ex-governor of a southwestern state who was a fiddler in a gambling hall. The younger men, and those who had done hard outdoor work in the past, were more successful at the diggings than the others. Men who were not accustomed to back-breaking labor found the rewards too small for their work in the creek beds and dry diggings. They went to find other jobs that they could do until they could get enough money put aside to return home.

Sometimes one did pick up a valuable nugget somewhere, but that was too uncertain a thing to be relied on. Charlie listened to strange tales of fortune and misfortune these days. "Was there ever," he thought, "any place on earth like this, where the odd and queer are the regular run of things, and the ordinary and routine are not known?" He shrugged his husky young shoulders and looked about for more entertainment.

They passed a long-legged Yankee holding a lock in his hand. He was calling out, through his nose, a description of the padlock. "Look a-here, this lock is a miracle of the whole entire universe. I'll wager any number of ounces of gold that nobody in this here crowd can open it in two minutes."

The boys pushed closer to watch. The miners were easy marks for anything on a Sunday in Coloma. They passed the lock from one to another. Everybody turned it and twisted it and shook it and hit it on something. Even Charlie took it, but could make nothing of the lock.

"Aw, let's go," muttered one of his friends in his ear. "It's nothing but a fake."

Then a rough-looking miner with a crop of black hair covering almost his entire face and chest took the lock with a bulldog expression in his fierce eyes. He tried and tried—and then it flew open. His face was comical with surprise and glee. He looked at the lock owner, who had turned his back to talk to somebody behind him and did not seem to see.

The hairy man gave a fat German next to him a shove, and whispered hoarsely, "Better make a bet, and I'll go halves." The German smiled happily, and the two men pushed forward.

The German put down his bag of gold dust, and the lock owner dropped beside it twenty Spanish doubloons. The gambler took out his turnip-sized watch. "Two minutes now," he cried, and the German started to work on the lock. He put his finger on the spring, as he had seen the hairy man do, and pushed and pushed, but it did not open.

"Your two minutes are up, my friend," drawled the Yankee through his nose, and pocketed the bag of gold and doubloons. With a look of complete dismay the German turned to the black-haired man—and found him gone. The crowd roared with laughter. The fierce-eyed fellow had been an accomplice, and these two crooks had taken in the sadder and wiser German to the extent of his last ounce of gold.

It was growing dark. "Listen," said Charlie. "That sounds like fiddling over there. Let's go."

A miners' ball was in full swing in a big tent, on a dirt floor packed as hard as earthenware. At one end stood a tall, rangy fellow with a fiddle held carelessly in the crook of his arm, sawing away. Overhead a row of oil lanterns jiggled and swung as the tent shook with the commotion.

When the tent was full the fiddler shifted his quid of tobacco, spat carefully across the floor, and sang out in a Kentucky twang:

"Now, gents, since we ain't got no ladies, we got to have a ball without 'em. All gents turn their rears this way." The miners roared with laughter and turned around. "All gents with canvas patches on the seats of their pants is to be ladies for the evening. Take your places."

He raised the fiddle and swung into "Buffalo Gals."

Buffalo gals, won't ye come out tonight—come out tonight—and dance by the light of the moon.

Each miner without patches grabbed a miner with patches, and they jigged and roared and howled and danced until the tent pegs shook.

"Do-si-do—around we go. Gent, take yo' gal by her lily-white hand."

Each patched miner held up his huge horny brown fist and had it grasped rudely by his partner, who swung him off the floor.

"Yippee!" squealed a short fellow with a goatee

beard, breaking loose and doing a fancy buck-and-wing jig in the middle of the floor.

Toward morning a man thrust his head in the door, and above the uproar he bellowed, "Everybody out! Dawn's a-bustin'."

The miners pulled on their coats and went to hunt their belongings. It was Monday. They moved out into the gray light, carrying their provisions, but without their gold. Now they were out to dig for more. In tents and shacks, gamblers and auctioneers and merchants counted their receipts and then locked them up in their safes.

13

Every Man for Himself

By the end of 1849, the better-known diggings were pretty well washed of gold, and the miners were wandering farther into the mountains searching out new claims. Major William Downie, formerly of the army, decided to prospect higher in the Sierras. Taking his men with him in the autumn, he found a steep-walled little canyon that looked promising. The major had working for him ten black sailors, an Irishman, an Indian, and a Kanaka. It made him smile to listen to his men, for they spoke in so many strange variations of the English language.

As the major walked about, smelling supper cooking over his campfire, he came upon a spot where somebody had been digging and panning gravel. He went back to the fire and announced, "We'll stay right here. This looks like gold country to me."

Next day he put several of the workers to digging into the icy gravel along the river, and the others to cutting logs and constructing cabins. Winter was close at hand, and the major felt he didn't have too much time to get established and stocked up for a long stay.

As they moved into the cabins, the whole crew began to sift the gravel on the sandbars. The major had been right. The panning they had done proved gold was there, and he thought that in the spring much of it would be found. But now he was worried about provisions for a permanent camp.

He called Jim, the South Sea islander, into the cabin and told him that he would have to go back to town to buy supplies, and to take nine of the men with him to pack the grub in. As Jim mounted his horse, his master gave him a bag of gold to pay for the food and told him to make the trip as quickly as possible.

Jim disappeared into the gray, swirling snow, and

the major frowned anxiously. "We'll have to hoard what provisions we have till it's time for them to come back," he said. "And they may be delayed by the drifts."

The ice thickened and the snow deepened so that it was impossible to pan for gold. But the men left in the canyon busied themselves chopping trees for fuel for their adobe fireplaces. The weeks passed, and no pack train with supplies appeared. Their little hoard of provisions dwindled until at last they were almost too weak from lack of food to get out of their bunks.

As the major lay in his cabin, he thought of the golden riches he felt sure were buried under this snow and ice.

Would he live long enough to dig it out?

Then one day he opened his eyes to see a blue sky and hear melted snow running in a small stream past his cabin. Ice was disappearing fast in the sun.

From far off a voice shouted, "Halloo! Halloo there! Major Downie!"

He got slowly up from his bunk and dragged himself to the door. As he pulled it open he saw an amazing sight. Jim, his dark Polynesian face wreathed in smiles, was riding through the canyon. Behind him came three mules loaded with provisions. There was no sight of the other nine men who had gone out with him. In fact, the major never did see them again. But behind

Jim trudged a laughing, shouting band of miners. They had gotten wind of the gold. Gold in Downie's Canyon! Here they came, picks and pans and crowbars swinging, bags of flour and beans in hand.

The major's cabins were soon the center of a camp called Downieville or The Forks. The hunch had been right. There was gold, and lots of it, too.

By the summer of 1850, the little rimmed-in basin, with its pure stream and thick green trees, was a tumble of dirty tents, shacks, holes, and piles of dirt and gravel.

Jim was faithful to his master. He panned gold by day, but took time off to cook the major's meals, and sometimes he went fishing for dinner. One evening he caught a big salmon. Showing it proudly to the major, he cried, "She big fish, Major. She weigh fourteen pounds."

He flung the fresh fish into a pot of water that he had scooped up from the river, and put it over the fire. When the fish was done, he poured off the water to remove the major's dinner and saw flakes of gold gleaming in the bottom of the pot. His eyes popped, and he ran to tell of this wonder.

A friend who had come to dine with the major remarked, "I've heard of the goose that laid the golden eggs, but never before of the fish that laid the golden nuggets!"

Gold was always coming to light in odd places. One night an old man came into camp hopping and kicking up his heels. Everybody thought at first that he had gotten hold of too much rum, but then they found that he was sober. He had been digging a hole for a tent pole and had discovered in it a pocket of fine gold.

Across the river, at Durgan's Flat, eighty thousand dollars' worth of gold was mined in the summer of 1850. Frank Anderson, the man who had first panned there, had left the signs that Major Downie first saw. When Anderson returned with his three companions, he took $12,900 worth from a claim only about sixty feet square.

Now it was becoming impossible to hire Indians or other workmen to do any mining. The workers deserted at once, and went to panning on their own. "Every man for himself" was the motto now. Claims were no longer unlimited in the richer areas. By general agreement, the first man to a claim had the right to a plot sixteen by forty feet, and measurements were taken. If he wished to move on, as he usually did after a short time, he sold his claim to a newcomer, who sometimes made a fortune out of it—but more often found it worthless.

There was a story going around the campfires that at a certain digging the men filled their tin cups with gold dust every day. The place was called Tin Cup Diggings, and miners for miles around left their claims to swarm there. But they found it no better than what they had left.

The placer miner was a restless man. He was here today and gone tomorrow. He lived on excitement, stirred up by stories of richer diggings beyond the next hill. The most restless miners were soon described as having "lump fever." Gold dust wasn't enough for them. Big lumps of gold were what they wanted. No sooner had they settled down to steady work on a claim than some wild story that a lump of gold had been found somewhere else would send them packing again.

Later the Chinese came to Downieville. They were quiet men who laughed good-naturedly among themselves, but looked with suspicion at the other miners. For the other miners had often tried to trick them into buying worthless claims. The Chinese worked hard, digging and panning, and tucked pokes of gold into their wide sleeves to be hoarded until the day when they could return to their own country as rich men.

Nearby were many other lively diggings and camps. There was Cutthroat Bar, Hoodoo, and Ranse Doddler. Here miners roared out their songs at night, after they had dried their pans of dust by the fire.

Oh, don't you remember sweet Betsey from Pike,
Who crossed the big mountains with her husband Ike,
With two yoke of cattle, a large yellow dog,
An old Shanghai rooster, and one spotted hog.

The lively words rose and bounced back from the walls of gulches and canyons.

Oh, what was your name in the States?
Was it Thompson, or Johnson, or Bates?
Did you murder your wife
And fly for your life?
Say, what was your name in the States?

14

The Gold Lake Stampede

In California, legends and tales about gold were becoming as thick as mosquitoes in the marshes on the San Joaquin River. Some of them were true. It was a fact that a ten-year-old boy named Perkins, in looking for a stone for his slingshot, picked up a nugget worth a thousand dollars. But it wasn't true that a prospector found a mountain made of solid gold and then died of excitement before he could hack it into nuggets. There wasn't much the miners didn't believe. They went about listening all the time for talk of rich diggings, where gold was so plentiful that it could be shoveled up without anyone's having to wash dirt out of it.

One day a gaunt, bearded man dragged himself into a mining-town camp and collapsed in front of the local theater. Nobody paid much attention at first. Everybody was busy in this town.

Nearby, two children were panning for gold in the street dust. They got a little from time to time, no doubt dropped carelessly by miners. They came closer.

"He's sick," said one boy. "I'll get my pa." He ran for his father, one of the few doctors in that part of the country. His father came at once and, turning the man over, said that he was nearly starved. There was also a strange wound on his heel. Passing miners carried the man to the hotel and wondered about him.

It was several days before he was able to talk, and then at first he didn't say much. However, one of his nurses, a burly miner himself, pricked up his ears when he heard the starved man whispering, "Gold, gold, gold. The lake. Look in the lake."

By the time the stranger had gotten well enough to sit up in a chair, his room was jammed with miners who sat on the floor and listened to his story. The man's name was Stoddard. He had come into California across the plains, and he and a friend had gotten lost from their group while crossing the Sierra Nevada. The two men had wandered for some days, living on the few rations they had with them pieced out with berries and nuts and an occasional squirrel.

One afternoon they climbed higher and higher into the mountains, so high they could see no signs of animal life anywhere about them. They had not crossed a stream for some time and were growing very thirsty, when Stoddard saw what he thought was a gleam of water through the huge pines. They ran toward it, and a beautiful placid lake burst into view.

"As we leaned down to fill our throats with the clear water, we thought of nothing at first but our thirst. Then when we had drunk all we needed I fixed my eyes on the strange water. Something was flashing and glistening down there in the sandy bottom," Stoddard related.

The two men scooped handfuls of the gravel up out of the water and found that it was more gold than sand. They sat back and stared at it. This was a golden lake. A lake of pure gold. There must be fabulous wealth in there! If they could only find their way out before they starved, and organize an expedition. They stood up. It was almost dark. The giant trees were disappearing into the blackness that was the forest behind the two men.

A sound! Nothing more than a whine. Then an arrow struck a tree beside Stoddard. Indians! They gazed frantically about them, reaching for their guns. Another arrow whined, and Stoddard's companion ran yelling into the forest. Stoddard whirled about and ran too. He felt a blow on his heel and stopped a moment as he saw the blood flowing. Then he ran again, forgetting any pain. He ran until he was exhausted, and toward morning just fell and slept where he was. When he woke up the sun was high. He could see no Indians and his companion had disappeared.

"I never saw him again. I don't know whether he starved or the Indians got him," said Stoddard. "But I wandered about till I found the trail leading here. That's my story. I found a lake of gold!"

The miners stared at each other, then shook their heads. This man was crazy. They talked about it a lot, but nobody believed Stoddard. When Stoddard was well again, however, he found twenty-five miners who agreed to form a company to share the gold. They decided to slip out quietly, so nobody else would know. But as they were moving out of town just before dawn, Stoddard turned and saw that they were being followed. Behind them came a group of miners so large that it looked as if the entire camp was trailing them.

When they got up into the high Sierras, the men asked Stoddard where the lake was to be found. Day after day they asked him. But after a while, when he only seemed confused, the men got angry. "What'll we do?" someone said. "Let's hang him." "No, give him twenty-four hours, then hang him if he ain't found this lake."

But during the night Stoddard sneaked quietly away and was not seen again for some weeks, when he turned up in another valley telling the same story. The baffled and angry miners dispersed slowly, going in different directions to various diggings. But they afterward called this expedition the Gold Lake Stampede, and the place where it ended, Humbug Valley.

Three quiet Germans who had joined the group went on alone, and found themselves, after a while, way up the Feather River. As they prepared to camp there the first night, one of them went to the stream for fresh water. He found a shallow bar from which he took up handfuls of gold. No Gold Lake—but here it was, riches in the Feather River! They started panning, and in four days took out about thirty-six thousand dollars in gold.

The first trip to town for supplies brought back a horde of miners. Bonanza! "I'm off for that rich bar in the Feather River. The richest yet." They came with picks. They came with pans. They came with rockers and long troughs, and some with only Mexican beans and spoons. They came from Poor Man's Creek, from

Nelson's Creek, from Hangtown, and Coloma, and Marysville, and San Francisco.

Before long the place had twenty-five thousand people in or around it. They came so fast and panned so much gold that the gravel bar was soon called officially Rich Bar. A man named Enoch Judson took out seven hundred fifty dollars in gold in one sack of dirt. Other miners took out so much gold that they agreed to allow the claims on the river to be only ten feet square. Farther away, however, the claims were to be forty feet square.

A crowd of Yankees arrived on the same day, and at the same place, as a big group of Frenchmen. They both tried to stake claims on the river, and both claimed the same spot. Fights started and knives flashed before one Yankee roared, "Look a-here, Frenchies, what do you say we settle this argument by a rip-roaring fight between one American and one Frenchman? And the loser takes his crowd off, leaving the claim to the winners."

The Frenchmen talked it over rapidly, and a spokesman agreed, "*Oui, oui,* messieurs. That we will agree to."

They each chose their champion, the toughest, roughest fighter in their gangs. Then the battle began, and a battle it was, for no holds were barred. At one moment the Frenchman was on top of the Yankee, punching, and his crowd roared. Next moment the American was delivering an uppercut to the jaw that caused the big Frenchman to stagger, and the Americans were leaping and shouting. At last, when the Yankee was punch-drunk and staggering on his feet, he knocked the Frenchman to the ground, and the defeated man lay there. The winners grabbed their picks and pans and rockers and made for their claim, howling for joy, while the French moved off, growling to themselves, but looking for a new claim.

Next day as the Americans were talking of their luck, a miner came up and told them that those Frenchmen who had gone down the river to stake out a new claim had struck the richest bonanza in all the valley.

These diggings were so exciting that others came besides miners. There was "Squire" Bonner, who called himself a judge. He put his "court" on wheels—he had a wagon—and with one book that looked heavy enough to be a law volume, he administered justice to all who would pay him. But he had to move on pretty frequently, as the miners caught on to the fact that he had no claim to judgeship and his services were not legal.

Of a different type was Charles Nahl. Coming to California in the early part of the rush, he soon gave up the idea of digging. He was an artist who had had first-class training in Europe. Now he lived in Marysville, where the Yuba and Feather rivers joined. From Marysville, Nahl traveled through the mining camps, sketching and painting. He drew the miner who washed his clothes of a Sunday, the miner who amused himself riding a horse wildly through the camp yelling, "Hunt your holes! I'm heading for you!" He drew the miner who found a treasure in the form of a good book and sat reading under the trees; and the homesick boy who spent his Sunday writing letters.

Once as he wandered through the diggings, he found a lonely grave on a hillside. Thrust into the dirt at the head was a pine slab with a little verse carved on it. He read:

A renegade cuss, here he lies;
Nobody laughs, nobody cries;
Where he's gone, how he fares,
Nobody knows, nobody cares!

15

The Mariposa

The little mission town of San Jose dozed in its afternoon siesta. Under a slanting porch roof slept a Mexican, his sombrero over his eyes. Nothing moved but a lazy dog scratching fleas. Into the dusty street rode a man, dark, slight, and erect in his saddle, wearing the clothing of the *Californio*, with jacket and sombrero.

He swung himself down from his horse before the little hotel with the lithe ease of the soldier.

A stranger in Eastern clothes standing on the steps of the hotel stared curiously at the newcomer. This easterner was Bayard Taylor, reporter for the New York *Tribune*.

Taylor watched as the horseman turned to his saddlebags and then called into the inn, "José, José, come and help me carry these bags."

A Mexican servant shambled through the door and grinned delightedly at the newcomer. "Ah, Colonel, sí—sí. José comes. At a moment's cry." He grasped one of the bags and carried it, back bent, into the hotel.

Bayard Taylor advanced, hand thrust out.

"Colonel Frémont! I thought I recognized your face. I should, for I have seen pictures of you often enough. May I tell you how happy I am to meet you here."

The colonel was in a great hurry, but in a courteous voice he greeted the easterner, shook hands with him, and talked a little while. Frémont was known as the Pathfinder of the West. He was the explorer who had journeyed through the uncharted wilderness with Kit Carson, the scout and guide. His reports of the great western lands, deserts, mountains, and rivers between the Mississippi Valley and the Pacific Ocean had helped the westward travelers. This was the Colonel Frémont who had come into California at the time of the war with Mexico and had done much to secure this territory for the United States.

The colonel ate a quick meal, clapped his western hat back on his head above his thin brown face, and rode off. He was heading toward Monterey, where his wife, Jessie Benton Frémont, and their little daughter, Lily, were living.

As he rode the colonel smiled. His bold yet quiet face seldom looked joyous or carefree. But now he was thinking of Jessie. She did not even know that he was coming. In 1847, they had bought a tract of land as an estate, paying three thousand dollars for it. Frémont had asked the American consul in Monterey to purchase a ranch for him, for he and Jessie wished to have a home in this newest territory.

Then in 1849, Jessie and Lily had made the hard trip across Panama and had landed in San Francisco. Colonel Frémont had found them there after he had survived a trip through the mountains, when many of his party had died of starvation and cold. And the news had come that the beautiful ranch they had counted on was nothing but a huge tract of wild land in the mountains.

"But how can we live there, John?" Jessie had stared

at him desperately. Very little money was left, and for all his fame the future looked dark to the colonel.

He answered, "I don't know, Jessie, but this tract has more than forty thousand acres in it—and it is in the country near the mining lands. Who knows? Perhaps there may be some gold there. On my way to California, I fell in with a party of miners coming up from Sonora, Mexico. I can try to make a deal with them. If there is gold on our Rancho de las Mariposas they will mine it, if I can supply them with food and tools and give them half of all they take out."

Jessie had decided that she and Lily would be happier out of brawling, noisy San Francisco, and so Frémont had placed them in two rooms in the home of a Mexican lady in Monterey.

The past few weeks had not been easy for the colonel. He had obtained credit from a friend in San Francisco and had bought provisions and tools for his Mexican miners. He had also purchased furniture and sent it down to Jessie.

Swinging down from his horse, he grasped a sack with both hands.

"Jessie, Jessie," he cried as he burst in the door. Then he stopped and looked around him appreciatively, for the rooms they rented from Señora Castro already looked like home. Jessie had tacked white curtains at the windows, and the glow of a fire in the hearth fell on small Lily stretched out on a grizzly-bear robe. Jessie Frémont looked up from her sewing. Never before had she seen her husband with that excited look in his eyes—no, not even when he told her of his fights with Indians, or of the time he crossed the snowy Sierra Nevada in midwinter.

He dumped the heavy sack before her and opened the top. She leaned forward, but could not speak.

"This is gold, Jessie. We are rich. My Mexican miners have dug more than seventy-five thousand dollars' worth of gold in a month up there on the Mariposa."

"You mean—we have all this gold?"

"All this and more, much more." He ran out and returned with two more bags of the same size. "In each of these sacks we have as much as twenty-five thousand dollars' worth of gold. And what is even better, this is only the surface gold. I am sure that there is quartz gold on the property, and that the mother lode runs through our land!"

Jessie felt dazed. She had just been worrying about their debts. Now they were to be multimillionaires!

Her husband was talking as he sat before the fire. "My dear, I have ordered a carriage for you. I heard that one is arriving by ship in San Francisco soon. We will get a team of good mules, and I shall take you to our Mariposa mines. We will camp under the trees, and you shall see the miners taking treasure from the streams and dry ravines."

"Father," asked Lily with curiosity, "what is mariposa?"

"*Mariposa* means butterfly in Spanish. The land is called that because on the slopes of the hills grow butterfly-shaped wild lilies."

When the child was asleep, dreaming of all these wonders, Jessie asked, "But John, where shall we keep all this gold?"

"Well—you must find a place."

"Then I guess I had better hide it."

Together they shoved the sacks under the beds. John Frémont soon went back to his mines. He was much troubled by the hordes of men tramping and riding to his property to dig up his gold. He knew that this placer mining could not last long, for it was taking only the surface gold. He meant to go back east when he had gathered enough gold. There he would buy a stock of machinery, hire engineers, and bring them back to sink shafts into the deep quartz deposit beneath.

But before the carriage arrived, Colonel Frémont received news that he had been elected to the Senate from the newest state—California. He arranged his affairs at the Mariposa mines and rode hastily down to Monterey. There Jessie and Lily, who had heard the news already, were happily packing to go back east.

The colonel found his wife trying to haul the heavy sacks of gold out from under the beds. She said, laughing: "I heard a story yesterday of a miner who hid his gold in a hollow tree, and when he went to get it found that squirrels had taken it all. He located some of it, buried in unlikely places, but never found it all. I am like the squirrels. I hid our gold and slept on top of it."

As the Frémonts went up to San Francisco and then prepared to take a ship for New York, Jessie wondered how many years it would be before she saw this strange and wonderful part of the world again. They would soon be multimillionaires, and with her famous husband in the Senate, they would live in Washington, she thought. But since California did not formally join the Union as the thirty-first state until September 9, 1850, Frémont's term as senator ran for only a few months, and he was not reelected. So Jessie returned to California sooner than she expected.

She did take those trips up into the wild hills that she and her husband had talked about, and she did live for a time in a small house on the Mariposa. But the Frémonts' dreams of gold came to little, for the colonel was a better explorer than a business manager. The miners flooded onto his Mariposa land until the gulches and streams and hills resembled battlegrounds.

The night of their departure for New York, John, Jessie, and Lily stood at the rail of the ship. Lily pointed to the city of San Francisco, where countless kerosene lamps shone from canvas dwellings, and said, "Look— the lighted tents of the town look like solid gold!"

16

Bandit!

Two rivers run down from the mining country to join
and flow together into upper San Francisco Bay. One
of these is the Sacramento, and the other the San
Joaquin.

On the banks of the Sacramento, seventy-five miles
upstream, is the city of Sacramento, and fifty miles up

the San Joaquin is Stockton. These were the gold rush towns, and all the miners arriving by sea headed for them. Bayard Taylor, writing to the New York *Tribune* in 1849, called Stockton a "canvas town of a thousand inhabitants and a port with twenty-five vessels at anchor!" He spoke of "the mingled noises of labor around—the click of hammers and the grating of saws—the shouts of mule drivers—the jingling of spurs—the jar and jostle of wares in the tents—"

But by the following year, Stockton had become the county capital. Five thousand people were living there, besides the drifting miners coming and going to and from the mother lode country.

One day the sheriff stood tacking a sign on a post. Several little boys drew closer to look curiously at the placard. A muleteer hitched his team and strolled over. It wasn't long before a crowd had gathered, all bending forward to read. Those who couldn't read asked their neighbors to spell out the sign for them. It read: REWARD FOR THE CAPTURE OF THE OUTLAW JOAQUÍN MURRIETA.

"Gosh," gasped one of the children, "that's the wildest outlaw in Californy. My pa says nobody's safe with Joaquín roaming loose."

"How long you been chasing Murrieta, Sheriff?" a man asked.

The sheriff finished nailing up the placard, turned, and pushed back his big hat. The small boys eyed him admiringly.

"Well, ever since I got my badge. Down at Murphy's Camp he was a three-card monte dealer in a gambling joint. It was then his brother was hanged for horse stealing. Joaquín tried to defend him, and the boys there flogged him with a cat-o'-nine-tails. Murrieta's been an outlaw ever since. He hates all gringos. But we'll get him." The sheriff strolled away.

Two or three others had joined the crowd while the sheriff had been talking. One of them was a Mexican rider, short and wiry, who rode up and reined in his horse. He looked as if he had spent his life in the saddle. He wore a scarlet sash about his waist, silver-mounted pistols on his hips, a black jacket, and tight trousers decorated with jingling silver ornaments. His big black sombrero was pulled down over his eyes.

Suddenly he leaned forward, catching sight of the sign, and spurred his horse into the crowd. The men and boys leaped back and stared open-mouthed. The Mexican drew in his horse so abruptly that it reared back on its hind legs. He drew a crayon from his pocket, leaned forward, and wrote in bold black letters across the placard: I WILL GIVE $10,000. JOAQUÍN.

Snatching his hat from his head and laughing with

a flash of white teeth, he waved the sombrero and galloped down the dusty street and out of town.

Not one of the tough miners so much as moved a muscle until the outlaw had disappeared in a cloud of dust. Nobody ever knew where Joaquín would appear, or when. A miner hiding his gold in his shack would hear a quick, quiet voice: "Lift your hands, señor. Now the gold. Hand it over!"

Or Joaquín would show up with his gang and his first lieutenant, Three-Fingered Jack, in the office of a store or saloon where gold was locked in a safe. "Open the safe, señores. So! Now the gold."

Joaquín and his men were pursued from one end of the gold country to the other, but never caught.

Law was slow in coming to California, but gradually towns were getting quieter with the appearance of families and sheriffs and courts. Churches and schools were being built. Posses of citizens were organized to hunt down outlaws. Many were caught and hanged. But where was Murrieta? Where next?

In the mother lode country, Mokelumne Hill—or Mok Hill as it was called by the miners—looked down on the Mokelumne and Calaveras rivers. It was a tough town, with a reputation for killings every weekend, when miners poured in from surrounding gold-producing gulches and streams. Nearby was Chinatown, where a thousand Chinese lived and dug gold and tried to keep out of trouble with the other miners who resented their coming to California.

One evening in the Zumwalt Saloon a card game was in progress. A stranger sat playing quietly, his hat pulled low. As often before, the talk got around to the outlaw Murrieta.

"Nobody can catch that Mexican," said one of the miners. "He's too slippery a customer. I'll bet he'll never be caught."

A young fellow across the table, who had been winning, laughed loudly and roared out, slapping down a poke of gold on the tabletop, "Here's betting I can shoot that Murrieta, if I ever come to see him!"

The stranger in Mexican clothes at the other side of the table pushed back his hat from black, glittering eyes. With a silver-mounted pistol in each hand, he jumped on the table.

"I am Murrieta. Kill me if you can!"

Every man in the room sat stiffly. There wasn't a sound from them. There wasn't a single movement. The Mexican laughed, leaped from the table, and strode out. They heard his horse's hoofs clattering out of town.

He passed through Angels Camp, and on to Los Muertos Creek. Los Muertos, or Creek of the Dead, was a camp of Chileans and Mexicans where English was scarcely understood at all. There the Murrieta gang held undisputed sway for two years. Then, in 1852, the state of California issued a reward of five thousand dollars for the capture of the famous bandit, and the California State Rangers went after him in earnest.

In July of the following year, the little camp of Los Muertos suddenly seemed deserted. Slowly riding into the dusty main street came a grim-looking group of men. In front rode Captain Harry Love, and behind him were twenty rangers.

The captain dismounted and began to question the Mexicans.

"Where's Joaquín?" he asked. "How long since you've seen Murrieta?"

"No speak English," was the only reply.

The captain asked in Spanish, "Where is Joaquín?" But the Mexicans shook their heads silently. Then Captain Love saw a woman whose eyes burned as he asked his question. This was La Molinera, the former wife of Joaquín, and she hated the bandit. She told the rangers to go to Priest Valley and they would probably find him. To mislead any of Murrieta's spies, Captain Love led his rangers south toward Los Angeles. Then as soon as it grew dark they doubled back to the ravine where the woman had said Joaquín might be hiding.

As the rangers approached they saw campfires burning down in the arroyo and heard laughter and singing in Spanish. They crept closer and closer, until Captain Love could see Three-Fingered Jack outlined against the flickering light. Then they closed in and the shooting started. Captain Love kept his eye on Three-Fingered Jack and followed him as he crashed through the underbrush. As the bandit turned to fire, the captain shot first and killed him.

Joaquín leaped for a horse and dashed, without saddle, out of the ravine. But one of the rangers, named Henderson, saw him and fired. The horse went down and the outlaw, leaping clear, ran toward the dark woods. Henderson fired again. Joaquín Murrieta, the most famed bandit of the gold country, fell dead.

Law was coming to the gold country, coming with the sheriffs and the posses at the point of a pistol. There were other bandits who were hunted through the arroyos and the mountains. Later there was Rattlesnake Dick and Black Bart. But no name was as widely known or held in as much dread as that of Murrieta. Songs were made about him, and as the miners sat at night about their fires, they beat on tin pans with knives and spoons and roared out the tune, "Joaquín Murrieta, the Bandit Chief!"

17
Hangtown

They suddenly stopped on a very high hill,
With wonder looked down on old Placerville;
Ike sighed when he said, and he cast his eyes down,
Sweet Betsey, my darling, we've got to Hangtown.

A wagon train was straggling into Placerville. A young man smiled as he heard one of his companions singing that song about "Sweet Betsey from Pike." He waved good-bye to his companions of the long road westward, for they were all separating now that they had arrived at their destination. Then he strode eagerly into the little mining town.

He was a young fellow named Studebaker, nineteen years old, blue-eyed, and strong looking, with gold fever in his bones. He had come from South Bend, Indiana. But he had Pennsylvania Dutch blood in his veins and in his speech, too. His hands were big and rough from the use of carpenters' tools. All he had owned had been lost in the crossing of the plains in this year 1853, at least all but fifty cents jingling in his dusty pants.

Although the town's name was Placerville, everybody called it Hangtown. It was a noisy place with tents and shacks scattered along a ravine beside a rushing stream. It was on the overland trail and the road from Coloma, so its main street was continually packed with wagons.

John Studebaker was out for gold, but he had no pick, no pan, no rocker—and no money to buy them. So he cast his eye about for a job and noticed a blacksmith's shop. It was a log cabin, half shop and half living quarters. There was a man inside pounding and hammering, glancing every now and then at the broken tools and wagons waiting to be repaired.

Studebaker strolled up and the man turned, barking out suddenly: "Young fellow, you got a likely look in your eye. Could be you're a blacksmith or a carpenter?"

"I might." The young man smiled, shifting his big shoulders against the doorjamb.

"Can you mend a wagon?"

"I might."

"Can you fix up a busted axle on a stagecoach, and mend miners' pans, and put handles on picks, and shoe a horse or mule?"

"I might."

"Can you make a wheelbarrow?"

"Sure."

"You got a job," said the man. "Come right in. My name is Hinds."

So John Studebaker went to work. He lived with his boss in the other side of the log house, where the entire furnishings consisted of two bunks, a stove, and several empty barrels to use for tables and chairs. At first he spent all of his work hours repairing wagons and coaches. Then he began to make wheelbarrows. His first attempt was so crude that Hinds burst out laughing. But Studebaker improved with experience, and before long he was known as Wheelbarrow Johnny, and the miners came to buy all he could make.

Studebaker soon felt at home in Hangtown. As he strolled about he passed the little butcher shop of Philip Armour, another young man who came for gold and stayed to start a business. And he stood for a while grinning, watching a tall skinny man called Mark Hopkins, who had driven his wagon up from Sacramento with a load of fresh vegetables to sell on the corner. Hopkins, a partner of Huntington, the storekeeper in Sacramento, had planted a vegetable garden near the river. His produce yield was so great that he sold what he could not eat. Hangtown was a good place to sell it, for the miners tramped into town famished for something besides Mexican beans and bacon and fried bread. They paid him oversize prices for his oversize turnips and squashes and tomatoes.

One night young Studebaker stretched his long legs out in his bunk and asked his boss, "Why do they call this place Hangtown?"

"Well, that's quite a story, young fellow. Bill Daylor and Perry McCoon used to farm up near Coloma before gold was found. When Marshall picked up the 'color' in the millrace, these two went panning. They had some Indians to help, and they found plenty of gold in this ravine, which they called the Old Dry Diggin's. Why, in one week they got about seventeen thousand dollars' worth of gold here. Prospectors came a-flocking. In 1850, fifty millions was taken out hereabouts."

"But what about the name?"

"Well, in '49 there was a crew of highwaymen hereabouts robbing miners of their gold. They called themselves the Owls. Now, you know this country was Mexican till '46, then a U.S. territory till '50. And there wasn't no law here to speak of. The Mexicans didn't need much, and so many came in with the gold rush that the law couldn't get here in time. Miners had to make their own law. If a man committed a little crime, he was run out of town or given thirty-nine lashes on the bare back with a cat-o'-nine-tails. But if he stole a horse or mule, or murdered his fellow creature, he was hanged. And if he stole a man's poke of gold, likewise.

"These Owls held up and robbed a Frenchman named Cailloux, who kept a store down the road, and took fifty ounces of gold. Next morning, three of 'em was taken and hanged from that big oak tree down there at the corner of Main and Coloma streets. Later, miners' courts were held for Irish Dick Crone and other rapscallions. So now, though Tom Nugent, our postmaster, says this town is officially named Placerville, everybody calls it Hangtown. But outlaws avoid it like it had rattlesnakes in it, and as we ain't got no other law, our kind keeps us peaceable."

"I think I'll go out prospecting now that I've got enough money to buy my gear," said Studebaker slowly. "I've got to try it."

"Sure, go ahead. But when you get tired of it, come on back. I've got a good job waiting for you. This is the first time I've felt fairly rested in a good long while."

"What's a placer?" Studebaker asked. "And what's this talk I heard over at the Golden Nugget Saloon about something called a long tom?"

"Placer is just a Spanish word meaning a gravel deposit on top of the ground. A long tom's a slanted wooden trough, sometimes as long as several hundred feet. Gravel is dumped in it and then washed by water. The long tom's got riffles, or strips of wood, like the rocker. Lately I've heard of some fellows getting mercury to put in to draw the gold out. A cuss came in and bought calomel pills, which has got mercury in them, to put in his rocker the other day.

"Some of these 'mud rats' go to coyoting," Hinds went on. "That's tunneling into a dry bank of dirt or gravel like a coyote does. They sometimes call it drifting, too. You drift into the bank from one side, and tunnel around in there instead of taking down the whole hillside, as some do. Not many make fortunes digging like a coyote or wading the creeks like mud turtles. You'll be back, young fellow."

But young Studebaker got his tools and his cooking

131

outfit and his rocker and went prospecting with the mob of other men. They were joined from day to day by more and more plodding in along the overland trail or coming up the Sacramento River from San Francisco.

As he was leaving town Studebaker passed a wagon train camped for the night. Several women sat about a fire, talking.

One woman was saying, "You ought to see the grand cheeses I used to make back in Ohio." Another tossed her head and bragged, "My rhubarb pies and plum jellies were the talk of my county back in Maine." Two others joined in. "You should have seen the quilt I made in my famous daisy pattern in Indiana," and "But my flannels in Iowa—"

There was a tall, thin, rawboned girl with straggly hair falling over her sunburned face from under a dirty sunbonnet, leaning against a tree nearby.

"Wal," she broke in, "I don't care a doggone for your old cheeses and pies and quilts and sich sort of Yankee fixin's. I'm from Pike County, Missouri—and I can cut up a hog, shoot a bear, and play cards." She swung her gun under her arm, reached for her frying pan, and strode off to head for the nearest diggings.

John Studebaker didn't pan for gold very long, for he found that it was harder work than he was used to and that it paid him less. He went back to Hangtown, and later on, when he had saved gold the miners paid him, he returned to South Bend, Indiana, and helped found the firm that made wagons and then automobiles. Like Mark Hopkins, who became one of the founders of the Union Pacific Railroad, and Philip Armour, the butcher, who started a meat-packing plant in Chicago, he made his fortune on California gold. But he didn't get it by digging it out of the earth with a pick and shovel.

18

A Song and a Dance

In the days of old, the days of gold, the days of '49!

So sang the miners in 1852. Already the days of '49 were "the good old days." After three years the towns were becoming "civilized," with women and children slowly drifting in, with schools and churches and law courts taking over. Yet the miners still came from everywhere.

And following the men with picks and shovels were musicians, actors, and dancers. Stories traveled fast—tales of gold showered on entertainers by enthusiastic gold diggers. Theatrical people left the showboats of the Mississippi to go west, they deserted the stages of Europe, New York, and Philadelphia, of New Orleans and Boston. They came across the plains in covered wagons, and carried their violins and carpetbags filled with costumes across the swamps of Panama.

The day that the much-talked-of, fiery Lola Montez arrived in Grass Valley the whole mining town turned out to gape. Lola was the Countess Landsfeld, and had left Europe after a revolution in which it was said that she had served as a spy. She had already danced in other mining camps, and some of the men at Grass Valley said they never saw anything like her famous Spider Dance.

Among those who watched for Lola to arrive was a small girl who looked no more than four years old though she was really six. Her bright eyes under a mop of red hair looked eagerly down the road when she heard the sound of a horse trotting along at a furious pace.

Into town rode the most beautiful lady this child

had ever seen. She was dressed in black velvet, with a white collar about her neck and a plumed hat swaying on her head. She leaped from her horse and swung her little riding whip in greeting. Behind her, at a slower pace, rode a tall man who frowned at the crowd and then quietly followed the exciting Lola into the house. But as they entered, Lola caught a glimpse of the small girl with the black eyes and red hair.

"Ah," she cried with the slight Spanish accent she always affected in a crowd. "The lovely leetle girl— who is she?"

"Lotta Crabtree," said the child shyly, ducking her head down.

"Come back to see me, Lotta. *Bonita*, you are *bonita*. Pretty."

As Lotta climbed into her chair at the long table in her mother's boardinghouse, where miners gobbled up the food, she thought of the pretty lady. The men were talking about her now too.

"Did you know that Lola Montez, the 'lady tiger,' has come to live in Grass Valley? Sure, she bought a cottage just around the corner. I saw her ride in. She got out of the stagecoach and came galloping in just for the effect, you know. Haw, haw, haw! She'll always do that. Did you see her husband? I'd hate to have to follow her around. Her name's not really

Montez, or Lola either. She was born Eliza Gilbert, in Ireland. But she's a countess now."

Mrs. Crabtree glanced at Lotta. She had never seen the child so excited, not even when her father left New York with the gold miners. And no, not even when she and Lotta had sailed to Panama, and then come up to San Francisco to this strange country themselves. Now Lotta's father was off in the mines, but he never had any luck, so his wife had to board miners.

Next day Lotta slipped away and ran to the cottage. She hung on the fence until the beautiful blue-eyed, dark-haired Lola Montez came out with a dog, a cat, and a big white parrot. As Lola noticed Lotta, she smiled and called her into the yard. The child approached slowly, but soon lost her shyness with this friendly actress.

As the days passed, Lotta became the constant companion of the famous countess. They rode horseback together over the green hills, looking up at the towering Sierra mountains, and watching with interest as new settlers planted orchards and wheat fields. They dismounted and picnicked in the grass where small flowers bloomed.

Soon Lola began to teach the child dance steps. She found her a very apt pupil. Little Lotta picked up fandangos, highland flings, and a few ballet steps immediately. But she was always especially delighted with jigs and reels. And when she danced them she was so taken by the rhythm that she laughed out loud as she danced.

From time to time Lola disappeared on a series of tours through the mining towns, dancing and coming back with sacks of gold. Her best dance was the spider number, where, toward the end, spiders made of India rubber and whalebone flew from her skirts into the audience.

The women of Grass Valley all liked Lola. She was so friendly and warm-hearted, and she wore calico dresses like theirs. Nothing uppity about Lola, even if she was a countess. She went to the sewing circle, and she always had a party for the few children of the town on Christmas.

But one day Lola came back from Marysville furious. She walked the floor like a tigress, as some people called her.

"I went to give my Spider Dance," she told Lotta. "But those miners did not want to see me. They threw eggs at me. I danced anyway. They yelled and shot off pistols. I shall leave this place and go to Australia."

Then Lotta went home to hear even more upsetting news. Her mother told her that her father had sent for them. So Lotta tearfully said good-bye to Lola Montez, and went with her mother by stagecoach and then on mules up steep mountain trails to Rabbit Creek.

Few mining camps were as hard to reach as Rabbit Creek. It perched on a little plateau under the shadow of a high mountain. The Crabtrees were no sooner settled than Mrs. Crabtree found that she must once again start taking boarders.

One day not long after their arrival, up the steep trail came the beautiful Lola. She had come to get Lotta. She wanted to take the little dancing girl with her to Australia. Mrs. Crabtree clamped her firm lips together after answering with a simple no, and that settled the matter.

Yet the child's mother could see that there was talent in this little girl. Lotta couldn't help dancing and singing. Mart Taylor, who kept the store and saloon, was an old-time actor, and he had built a small log theater in Rabbit Creek. It wasn't long before Lotta was kicking up her heels in jigs and reels, bringing showers of golden nuggets and Mexican dollars onto the stage.

Mrs. Crabtree, for all her prim ways, was delighted. And when Mart Taylor told her of a plan he had for a wandering troupe, with Lotta as the child star, Mrs.

Crabtree agreed. She even learned to play the triangle and taught Lotta a few more songs.

The last performance in Rabbit Hill was a triumph for the lively little girl. She did an Irish jig. Her costume was green: knee breeches and jacket, and a high green hat. She swung a small shillelagh in her hand. Behind the flickering candles set up in empty bottles for footlights, Lotta flung her red hair back and laughed as she danced. The miners roared approval, and when she sang "How Can I Leave Thee" they wept, thinking of home and mother. Mrs. Crabtree had to bring a basket on the stage to gather up the gold.

The trip through mining camps was a rough one. The players hitched their mules together, and crept up and down steep trails that were so frightening that Lotta and her mother had to close their eyes. At times they had to lie on the floor to avoid bullets because a fight had broken out in the hall.

Lotta danced in Hangtown, in Marysville, in Chinese Camp, in Hornitos, in the Mariposa mines, in Stockton, Sacramento, San Francisco, and in Downieville. She became the pet of the mining camps, and men walked miles to town to see her.

When boom days in the diggings were over, Lotta was still a favorite in the theaters in the cities. As she grew older, Lotta Crabtree became known from coast to coast. The miners who went back home talked of her, for she had touched their hearts with her songs and made them laugh with her dances. They never forgot the child with her mop of red hair whose face crinkled in an impish grin as she did a hornpipe or kicked up her feet in a jig and reel.

19

The Golden Dream

After 1854, placer gold began to give out. Men with gold fever still poured into California, but they met as many others who were leaving. Panning gold no longer paid everyday expenses, even though prices had gone down. Now gold mining was being done in a big way. Gold dredgers plowed up the rivers. Engineers came in to install mining machinery for deep-shaft quartz mining. (Between 1849 and 1859, California was mined of almost six hundred million dollars' worth of gold.)

Many of the miners went into other work, and became citizens of California. Others went back east. In ten years the population of California had increased from fifteen thousand to nearly four hundred thousand. Only a few hundred men made fortunes from gold. But others profited from the gold that moved rapidly from the miners' pockets into the pockets of lawyers, bankers, real estate men, and storekeepers.

The gold rush had made San Francisco one of the important cities of the world. Wells Fargo stagecoaches rattled over rough mining camp roads. Later, Stanford, Huntington, Hopkins, and Crocker built the Union Pacific Railroad to join west with east.

Old John Sutter spent his life trying to get justice. He died at last in Washington, still striving to bring his claims to the attention of the United States government. For him, gold was "bad medicine." For the Indians, it was bad medicine too. The white men hired them, then ruined them with drink or drove them from their forests and streams.

For James Marshall, in particular, gold was bad medicine. For years the man who became famous as the first to find gold lived in a cabin not far from the mill site at Coloma. He dug for gold and panned it out. But his luck was bad. He never found enough to make him prosperous, and he ended his life a strange old man who continually mumbled about gold.

Famous people journeyed out to the gold fields. There was Horace Greeley, the editor of the New York *Tribune*, who traveled out by stagecoach.

Mark Twain, who later wrote *Huckleberry Finn*, went to California not long after the Civil War, and lived in a little cabin on Jackass Hill. This was at a time when towns and camps were already being deserted in California. Deep shafts were beginning to go down into the earth of the mother lode country, to take out gold quartz. Stamp mills were being built to crush the ore. Wing dams and flumes were changing whole riverbeds.

It was in Angels Camp that Mark Twain heard the joke that became his famous story "The Jumping Frog of Calaveras County." With this ridiculous yarn he set the whole world laughing.

Bayard Taylor, the reporter, recorded his gold rush adventures in a book called *Eldorado*.

Eventually ghost towns were everywhere, all through the mother lode land. On the porches, behind posts where horses and mules had so recently been tied all day, sat old-timers swapping yarns.

"Remember the trip around the Horn, when we

thought the leaky tub would sink to Davy Jones's locker?"

"And the fevers of Panama, and the parrots screaming in the jungles?"

"Remember the boys from the plains, coming down the Sierras with hungry wild eyes, and the gold fever in their aching bones?"

"Sure do. And the gamblers in the tents, slicker'n hog fat? And the highwaymen on the roads—recall Joaquín Murrieta? And Rattlesnake Dick? Then there were the troupers of the shanty theaters. I saw Edwin Booth once, over in Angels Camp. And I watched Lola Montez dance the Spider Dance, and fill her slipper with gold. There was little carrot-top Lotta Crabtree, too—and you know they say she's the hit of the east coast now!"

"Remember the camps—Git-Up-And-Git, You Bet, Ground Hog's Glory, Dead Mule Canyon, Gospel Gulch, Shirt-Tail Canyon, Sailor's Slide, and Chucklehead Diggings?"

"Yep. I recollect the cold nights and the hot days, too. I can smell bacon and frijoles, and hear the boys coming in at sunset, a-roarin' and a-yellin' out songs."

Then a cracked voice would begin to sing, "Oh! Susanna, now don't you cry for me, for I'm off to Cal-i-for-ni-a, with a tin pan on my knee!"

The old-timers would tip their split-bottomed chairs back against the decrepit wall of the Last Chance Saloon and grin sociably at one another.

"Say, you ever hear of that nugget a man called Hance found while he was chasing a stray mule down at Carson Hill? He got a chunk weighing fourteen pounds. It was at Carson Hill that the biggest nugget ever found in America came out. It weighed a hundred and ninety-five pounds and was worth over forty thousand dollars!"

These old-timers hadn't gotten much gold in the hills of this gleaming land. They ended up with not much more than the clothes they wore. But like every miner who came and dug and sang and skylarked in the land of gold, they had adventure and comradeship and excitement to remember. All across America, doctors, carpenters, politicians, merchants, dentists, writers, musicians—all who had been Forty-Niners— had memories they would not have traded for the gold they had not kept.

And the old-timers still had, at the back of their minds, a thought that they wouldn't admit. They still went out secretly for a little digging now and then. "Maybe I'll find a nugget—maybe I'll get lump gold." They had that gleam in the eyes—the golden dream that had brought men from Germany, Peru, China,

Scotland, and all parts of the United States out to this wild and wonderful land. Gold! In California. "What's California? That's where the gold is!"

This Book
Belongs to

Garrett
Rietveld